ENDORS

I am happy to endorse Shawn's book. planted him to be a blessing to the women of God in his church and all over the world. He believes there is neither male nor female in the Spirit of God, and God wants to use everyone who wants Him to bring them to their salvation to know His death, burial, and resurrection. Shawn has prayed for me and has spoken life to me concerning the ministry God has called me for. He prophesizes and speaks wisdom to my spirit. I know God is going to use him to bring many to Jesus Christ. God has shown me many young men following him to the altar. His book will bless this world through the people of God. This young man loves his family and people. He is not ashamed of the Gospel of God. He appreciates where God has brought him from. He has a heart and hands pulling others to their purpose with the confidence of our Lord Jesus.

Judith C. Plater
Owner of New Image Beauty Salon

Shawn Easton's book; 'Eagles and Mountains' obviously reveals his personal prophetic quests for changes within the Church at large. He brings up answers to questions most people would never think of asking. His book will stretch your level of interest into the multiple areas of God's thoughts and desires for changes need in present day Church. It's a timely piece of work.

Kent Simpson
Apostolic Prophet and Founder, Prophetic Ministries Today

EAGLES AND
MOUNTAINS

VOLUME I

Convergent Identity in the
4 Face Heavenly Government

INCLUDED WITH
INTERACTIVE ACTIVATIONS

SHAWN EASTON

CONTENTS

ACKNOWLEDGEMENTS

I am grateful to my loving and supportive wife Keisha and our wonderful children, Josiah, Joshua, Talya, and Nikolas. Thank you for your love, support, prayers, encouragement, and the continuous inquiries on the progression of this book. When I see and think of you all, it motivates me to passionately pursue the Lord even more, to lay a foundation for you all to build upon so you may change your generation.

I thank my parents, Bishop Darnell and First Lady Margo Easton for your encouragement, prayers, and for the spiritual legacy you continue to lay for me, our family and many others.

I would like to thank Pastor David and Tracy Whittington for your continued encouragement, words of affirmation and identity that has been spoken into my life.

Thank you to Brother George Harrod and Brother Harry Harrod for your encouraging words which assisted in drawing this book out from the wells that is within me, as you continually asked when the second book was coming out. Thank you to Anita Britt for the time you put into proofreading the manuscript, and Jack Minor for your amazing editorial services.

Lord Jesus, I thank you for your grace and your love, and I thank you for the scribe angel you assigned to help and assist me in this endeavor.

INTRODUCTION

This book was born out of my continuous journey of discovery as I sought to fill my hunger to pursue the Lord; this craving and desire led me to seek and walk the ancient paths nonstop, the paths less trodden. This project is for the trailblazers and forerunners who boldly refuse to go on the trampled path, which seems to be easier because the weeds, grass and scrubs have been flattened and the earth has been packed down by the many footsteps left behind by those subscribing to the religious status quo, preventing ruts and providing a smooth ride that does not upset the status quo. Instead, these trailblazers are not afraid to launch out into the deep, choosing to walk in honor to the Lord and those who have gone before us, whatever the cost, including the ultimate cost of martyrdom.

If you feel a deep craving and yearning call within that seeks to connect to the corresponding deep craving and yearning call from our Heavenly Father, this book is for you. Somehow, you know internally there is more to God than what you have experienced thus far in your life. There is an inner holy hunger driving you to pursue the things of God like never before. This craving goes beyond simply taking another person's word about knowing God, but instead causes you to use the biblical teaching and experiences of others as a motivational stepping stone in pursuing your own encounter with our Living God so you might bring down Heaven to Earth.

During my early times of receiving concepts for this book, which I call downloads, I would look up and see eagles flying over me. One time, while getting inspirational downloads and promptings from the Lord regarding writing this book, another eagle flew low over me while I was driving. I don't recommend you take your eyes off the road to observe a flying eagle, but when this eagle flew over my head the Lord reminded me it was a loving sign to confirm his wanting me to write this book as I continued to seek Him.

I ask that you keep an open mind as you read this book and ask the Holy Spirit to reveal whatever He desires you to have. I believe the Lord is inviting and lovingly challenging us into a deeper walk of intimacy and a more exciting journey with Him, until Christ is formed in us!

My little children, for whom I am again in the anguish of childbirth until Christ is formed in you! (Galatians 4:19 ESV)

God Bless!

Shawn

CHAPTER 1
GIVE ME MY MOUNTAIN (GOVERNMENT)

*"Now therefore, **give me this mountain** of which the Lord spoke in that day; for you heard in that day how the Anakim were there, and that the cities were great and fortified. It may be that the Lord will be with me, and I shall be able to drive them out as the Lord said." And Joshua blessed him, and gave Hebron to Caleb the son of Jephunneh as an inheritance. Hebron therefore became **the inheritance** of Caleb the son of Jephunneh the Kenizzite to this day, because he wholly followed the Lord God of Israel. And **the name** of Hebron formerly was Kirjath Arba (Arba was the greatest man among the Anakim). **Then the land had rest from war.** (Joshua 14:12-15)*

God receives pleasure and joy from all His creation, whether it's the various angelic beings, oceans, trees, the exotic fish that swim in the various oceans, or any other thing He has created, including his crown jewel of creation, humanity. God receives praise and glory from the largest animal in the ocean, the blue whale, all the way to the microscopic sized Rotifer which is impossible to see with the naked human eye, all the way to the most complex creation in the cosmos... a born again human being.

First, let's establish that everything God creates, He loves. He initially created a variety of things on the earth for man to enjoy. In fact, in Genesis 2:19, God brought all the animals to Adam then sat back and watched with interest to see what he would name them. When His creation functions the way it was designed, it brings pleasure to God. In this chapter I would like to focus on one particular creation of God that he often speaks about in His Word, and that is mountains.

Most geologists classify a **mountain** as a landform that rises at least 1,000 feet (300 meters) or more above its surrounding area.

MOUNTAINS REFER TO GOVERNMENT

*Now it shall come to pass in the latter days That the mountain of the Lord's house Shall be established **on the top** of the mountains, And shall be **exalted above** the hills; And all nations shall flow to it. Many people shall come and say, "Come, and let us go up to the mountain of the Lord, To the house of the God of Jacob; He will teach us His ways, And we shall walk in His paths." For out of Zion shall go forth the law, And the word of the Lord from Jerusalem.* (Isaiah 2:2-3)

This passage shows the supremacy of the mountain (government or Kingdom) of the Lord, compared to other mountains (earthly governments). It says God's government will be on top of the other governments and shall be exalted above the hills (smaller governments). Hills are similar to mountains, a smaller version if you will; and they also can represent government.

A good comparison is to compare the Great Smoky Mountains to the Rocky Mountains. Both qualify as mountains based on the definition we listed above. However, despite having the name "Great" as part of its title, the Smokies have a maximum height of 6,643 feet at Clingmans Dome. By contrast, Mt. Elbert in the Rockies has a height of 14,400 feet, and that is just one of Colorado's 53 "fourteeners." So we can agree that the Rocky Mountains are at a much higher altitude than the Great Smoky Mountains. As a result, Colorado residents refer to the Smokies as the Smokey Hills, even though Tennessee residents would disagree.

Likewise, God's government will also be highly exalted above all other governments. And because God's Kingdom will be the supreme government, verse three says that many people shall come and say, "*come and let's go up to the mountain of the Lord"* (government of God). In God's government and Kingdom, He will teach them His ways and they will walk in His ancient paths.

Let's examine another scriptural account that involves mountains. This one involves the prophet Daniel telling King Nebuchadnezzar his dream and its interpretation, something all the wise men of Babylon were unable to do:

*"You, O king, were watching; and behold, a great image! This great image, whose splendor was excellent, stood before you; and its form was awesome. This image's head was of fine gold, its chest and arms of silver, its belly and thighs of bronze, its legs of iron, its feet partly of iron and partly of clay. **You watched while a stone was cut out without hands**, which struck the image on its feet of iron and clay, and broke them in pieces. Then the iron, the clay, the bronze, the silver, and the gold were crushed together, and became like chaff from the summer threshing floors; the wind carried them away so that no trace of them was found. **And the stone that struck the image became a great mountain and filled the whole earth.** "This is the dream. Now we will tell the interpretation of it before the king. You, O king, are a king of kings. For the **God of heaven has given you a kingdom**, power, strength, and glory; and wherever the children of men dwell, or the beasts of the field and the birds of the heaven, He has given them into your hand, and has made you ruler over them all—you are this head of gold. But after you shall arise **another kingdom** inferior to yours; then another, **a third kingdom** of bronze, which shall rule over all the earth. And **the fourth kingdom** shall be as strong as iron, inasmuch as iron breaks in pieces and shatters everything; and like iron that crushes, **that kingdom** will break in pieces and crush all the others. Whereas you saw the feet and toes, partly of potter's clay and partly of iron, the kingdom shall be divided; yet the strength of the iron shall be in it, just as you saw the iron mixed with ceramic clay. And as the toes of the feet were partly of iron and partly of clay, so **the kingdom** shall be partly strong and partly fragile. As you saw iron mixed with ceramic clay, they will mingle with the seed of men; but they will not adhere to one another, just as iron does not mix with clay.*

3

And in the days of these kings the God of heaven will set up a kingdom which shall never be destroyed; and the kingdom shall not be left to other people; it shall break in pieces and consume all these kingdoms, and it shall stand forever. Inasmuch as you saw that the stone was cut out of the mountain without hands, and that it broke in pieces the iron, the bronze, the clay, the silver, and the gold—*the great God has made known to the king what will come to pass after this. The dream is certain, and its interpretation is sure."* (Daniel 2:31-45)

In Nebuchadnezzar's dream, the king saw an awesome image which represented four powerful kingdoms that would be established in the earth. Then, in verse 35, he saw a stone not cut with hands come down and violently strike the image, utterly demolishing it. This unstoppable stone represents Jesus Christ. I would like to point out that it says the stone was cut out of the mountain without hands, showing the Heavenly and supernatural deity of Christ as the Son of God. This is the very stone that the builders rejected and refused, but it became the most important stone in the building.

The very stone the masons rejected as flawed turned out to be the most important capstone of the arch, holding up the very house of God (Psalm 118:22 TPT).

After this, the stone grew into a large mountain (Kingdom). What was noteworthy was that this stone was cut without the hands of man, making it supernatural. In this account the mountain represented the Kingdom of God, and I believe this supernatural stone was carved out of the heavenly Mount Zion.

But you have come to Mount Zion and to the city of the living God, the heavenly Jerusalem, to an innumerable company of angels, to the general assembly and church of the firstborn who are registered in heaven, to God the Judge of all, to the spirits of just men made perfect, to Jesus the Mediator of the new covenant, and to the blood of sprinkling that speaks better things than that of Abel. Hebrews 12:22-24

THE KINGDOM OF GOD RULES AND REIGNS IN THE EARTH FOREVER

Of the increase of His government and peace There will be no end, Upon the throne of David and over His kingdom, To order it and establish it with judgment and justice From that time forward, even forever. The zeal of the Lord of hosts will perform this. (Isaiah 9:7)

Arise, shine, for your light has come, and the glory of the Lord has risen upon you. For behold, darkness shall cover the earth, and thick darkness the people; but the Lord will arise upon you, and his glory will be seen upon you. And nations shall come to your light, and kings to the brightness of your rising. (Isaiah 60:1-3)

After King David won his battle over the Jebusites in 2 Samuel 5 at the fortress, Mount Zion, he renamed it as "The City of David," where it became the headquarters for David's military government. This area became the highest part of the site of Solomon's Temple, that was dedicated to God and where God came down and manifested His Shekinah glory.

We realize the enemy can only destroy, he can never create. We see this in Exodus 8 when God sent Pharoah the plague of the lice. For every previous miracle, Pharaoh's magicians were able to duplicate Moses and Aaron, but Exodus 8:18 says, "And the magicians did so with their enchantments to bring forth lice, but they could not." This is because this miracle involved creating life. The enemy longs and covets to have the ability to create like God, and in his jealousy over not having this power, he strives to deceive man into surrendering something to him that God created, to corrupt and twist its righteous function into something unrighteous.

> **SIDENOTE:** That's another reason why Satan hates and despises us so much. We not only took his place as praisers and worshippers of God, we also can co-create "with" God; something the enemy desperately desires to do but will never be able to do. And because of that, he despises the children of God with a passionate jealousy. Praise God!

Before God created man, the Bible shows us that He had a special place for mountains, even before Lucifer's rebellion in heaven. Notice what Lucifer said in his prideful heart. Notice it occurred while he was in heaven.

*"How you are fallen from heaven, O lucifer, son of the morning! How you are cut down to the ground, You who weakened the nations! For you have said in your heart: 'I will ascend into heaven, I will exalt my throne above the stars of God; I will also sit on the **mount** of the congregation On the farthest sides of the north; I will ascend above the heights of the clouds, I will be like the Most High.'* (Isaiah 14:12-14)

There was a mountain of the congregation that Lucifer desired to sit upon so he would be like the Most High God. This shows that even before Adam was formed, God had a fondness for mountains, even in the heavenly realms.

Since Lucifer couldn't sit on the mountain, of the congregation in heavenly places, he rebelled against God and now he is constantly attempting to sit and reign on the mountains in the earth, which, in actuality, are spiritual portals of authority and dominion that affect the natural realm within that area. Let's go a little further as we examine the plan of the enemy as it relates to mountains.

> SIDENOTE: Anything that God creates for His pleasure, the devil will attempt to steal and corrupt, using it in the realm of darkness. These things he covets and steals are of great value to the Kingdom of God, making it a tremendous threat to Satan and his realm.

MOUNT OLYMPUS

Mount Olympus, located in the Olympus mountain range, is the highest mountain in Greece. Around 700 BC, the ancient Greeks believed this mountain to be the home of the "gods." The Greeks were a polytheistic society that believed in many gods that made their abodes in this "mountain." Mount Olympus was supposedly the "seat" of the gods in Greek mythology. A seat is a very important term regarding government, and we will go further into this later.

Growing up, I was fascinated with Greek mythology. Mount Olympus is the location where their twelve gods and goddesses were supposed to sit and live. One of the meanings of the number twelve in the Bible is to represent government. Hmm, is this just a coincidence? I don't think so. We always need to remember that the devil is a corrupter of the righteous things of God.

THE GIANTS, NEPHILIM IN BIBLICAL TIMES

The giants, the Nephilim in biblical times, were drawn to the mountains and used them as their dwelling places when they took over a territory or region. The giants knew these mountains were areas on the earth that represented dominion, authority and rule in the spirit realm. They also realized there was an historic connection between their fallen angelic ancestors and the mountains.

The Book of Enoch is **not** a part of our biblical canon (collection of books in the Bible) today. However, it is in the canon of the Ethiopian Orthodox Tewahedo Church and the Eritrean Orthodox Tewahedo Church. Many of the early church Fathers felt that the early part of the Book of Enoch was rejected by the Jews due to its prophecies of Jesus Christ. Many Jews have a respect for the book and use it for reference and historical purposes, and consider it one of their holy books.

So I re-emphasize, it is not in our current biblical cannon. Despite this, the reason I am mentioning the Book of Enoch is because in the beginning, it goes into detail of how 200 Watchers (angels) fell from their place in God and went after women in the earth. This is referenced in Genesis 6 in the Bible. The Book of Enoch goes on to share how these 200 Watchers rebelled against God, then met on "Mount Hermon" to discuss their evil strategies to pollute the human bloodline to abort the coming of Jesus. The reason I bring this up is because it referenced the watcher angels'

7

meeting and discussing their strategies on a mountain (Mount Hermon), which would have been a place of dominion and government on the earth at that time.

Joshua 13:1-13 references many tribes of giants who inhabited and occupied this particular area. And you will notice that these areas in the scripture also included Mount Hermon and the surrounding area.

THE HIGH PLACES

Our first biblical account of an altar being located in the mountains occurs in Genesis 22 where God wanted to test Abraham's faith. We must also keep in mind that this took place prior to God giving Moses the law of commandments, including the one commanding Israel to not be like the pagan nations in performing human sacrifices. The main point of this reference is that it shows God telling Abraham to take Isaac and go to the land of Moriah and perform a burnt offering on one of the mountains that God would choose, which ended up being Mount Moriah. After Abraham passed this test of faith, God provided a ram to use for a burnt offering on the mountain. This act of obedience from Abraham AND Isaac set many governmental things in motion, in the spirit realm. This affects many people and nations today including Israel, the Body of Christ, and many Muslim nations which are turning to Christ because of the covenant between Abraham and God (in verses 8-9 Isaac also willfully submitted to Abraham and God during this test on the mountain because he was old enough to resist). This act of faith on Mount Moriah placed a special government over Abraham that positioned him to be the heir of the world.

For the promise to Abraham and his offspring that he would be heir of the world did not come through the law but through the righteousness of faith. (Romans 4:13 ESV)

DEMOLISH THE DEMONIC (CARNAL) HIGH PLACES

Now the Lord spoke to Moses in the plains of Moab by the Jordan, across from Jericho, saying, "Speak to the children of Israel, and say to them: 'When you have crossed the Jordan into the land of Canaan, then you shall drive out all the inhabitants of the land from before you, destroy all their engraved stones, destroy all their molded images, and demolish all their high places; you shall dispossess the inhabitants of the land and dwell in it, for I have given you the land to possess. (Numbers 33:50-53)

God gave Moses commandments to obey, and one of them included demolishing and destroying all the pagan high places, without exception. The high places were the areas where the people made sacrifices to their false gods. Notice that one of the things that God required Moses to do, in the above scriptures, in order to "possess" the land or to take authority over it, was to first demolish the pagan high places in the land. If the pagan high places would have remained, they would have hindered or possibly stopped the children of Israel from possessing the land. These pagan high places gave the demonic spirits legality and legal access to the land to set up their demonic government and strongholds. Keep in mind that the word 'legality' is a governmental word.

Many times in the Old Testament, when a righteous king followed an evil king that served false gods, the people of Israel would repent, (change their mind back toward the God of Israel) and be in need of revival and reformation in the land. To fully satisfy this need, one of the first things the newly righteous king would do is tear down the idols and altars of the false gods that were in the high *places.*

He also took out of all the cities of Judah the high places and the incense altars. And the kingdom had rest under him. (2 Chronicles 14:5)

Many times, these altars were located in the hilltops or mountains but some were in other areas. However, the altars in the mountains and hilltops were the ones most frequently used for sacrifices.

THE MOUNTAIN'S ALTAR IS LOCATED AT THE SEAT OF AUTHORITY

When it comes to the things of God, Satan and the realm of darkness are copycats. Satan steals a truth of light and a reality God created, then corrupts and tries to sell it as his own idea. The enemy will sell it to anyone who is open. This gullibility enables Satan to deceive man into thinking it is his own idea. Such is the case of the high places. Up to this point we have discussed that the high place is where the "altar" of that mountain (government) resides. Also, where the altar resides, the seat of authority of that spiritual entity, evil or godly (God) is revealed.

*And to the angel of the church in Pergamos write, These things says He who has the sharp two-edged sword: "I know your works, and where you dwell, where satan's **throne** is. And you hold fast to My name, and did not deny My faith even in the days in which Antipas was My faithful martyr, who was killed among you, where satan dwells."* (Revelation 2:12-13)

Things that are God-ordained and God-created have a Kingdom governmental mountain associated with it in the spirit realm. When that particular supernatural Kingdom governmental mountain is established in the earth realm, it is God's intent that all its infrastructure and assets will yield to God for Him to work through it (the spiritual mountain) for His glory. This would include businesses, churches, sheep nations (nations yielded to Christ's agenda), and ministries birthed and operating from heaven. Not every church or ministry on the earth is God-ordained. Some were first initiated and established in heaven, but due to continued disobedience and refusal to yield to heaven, they have been demoted and sat down in the spirit, even if it still seems to be running successfully on earth. Such was the church of Pergamos in Revelation 2. The Lord addressed the angel of the church; indicating there was a remnant of believers still there. They started out with Christ sitting on the seat of authority (the throne), but as they took themselves off the altar of surrender on top of that mountain, their allegiance transitioned to the enemy, leading to Satan sitting on the seat of authority of the church of Pergamos.

This tells us that we can start out submitting to the Lord, but if we become careless and cease abiding in Him in unwavering surrender, it can open a door for the enemy to take over that mountain (government). A throne is a seat of authority, because it is an extension and representation of the person or being of authority that sits on that throne. Physically, the high places were usually built toward the top of a mountain or in the highest land terrain of that region. This was seen in the Old Testament and it is still true to this day in the occult. In like manner, in the spirit realm the throne of that high place was also at the very top of that spiritual mountain.

This gives us some insight on why the evil giants in the Old Testament resided in the high mountains, because through the altar and seat of authority they would influence that region. As the giants "occupied" those mountains, the evil demonic forces who lived through the giants sat on the thrones in the spirit realm. The children of Israel realized and recognized this revealed truth regarding the connection between mountains and government. This is why God gave them a mandate to eradicate this race of giants along with their corrupted bloodline. By doing so, God's people would dislodge the giants from the mountains (government), driving the demonic forces out of that territory (land). Caleb realized this spiritual reality.

ACTIVATION:

This is an activation of framing a foundation in our spirit and mind, which we will build upon while we travel along on this journey as we go further in this book.

In this activation After reading this, close your natural eyes and open the eyes of your imagination and intentionally see your mountain, I am not going to tell you how it will look. For some it could be snow capped at the top, it could be full of fire, or engulfed in the glory cloud, it may be a different color or multiple colors than the mountains on earth. On this mountain I want you to see two things at the top. I want you to see a throne and beside the throne an altar. At this time no one is sitting on the throne and nothing is on the altar Get a journal or notebook and write down (journal) what you see, any details of the mountain, the details of the unseated throne, and the details of the empty altar. Also, if you heard anything journal that also. I want you to verbally say this to the Lord, "Lord I receive my mountain, my government, and I surrender my seat of authority, and the altar of my mountain to you, in Jesus' Name."

In your devotional time, I encourage you to read and meditate on Exodus 19:16-20, always covering your mind and imagination with the blood of Jesus, believing and decreeing that you have eyes to see, ears to hear and a heart to understand.

CALEB: GIVE ME MY MOUNTAIN (GOVERNMENT)

And now, behold, the Lord has kept me alive, as He said, these forty-five years, ever since the Lord spoke this word to Moses while Israel wandered in the wilderness; and now, here I am this day, eighty-five years old. As yet I am as strong this day as on the day that Moses sent me; just as my strength was then, so now is my strength for war, both for going out and for coming in. Now therefore, give me this mountain of which the Lord spoke in that day; for you heard in that day how the Anakim were there, and that the cities were great and fortified. It may be that the Lord will be with me, and I shall be able to drive them out as the Lord said." And Joshua blessed him, and gave Hebron to Caleb the son of Jephunneh as an inheritance. Hebron therefore became the inheritance of Caleb the son of Jephunneh the Kenizzite to this day, because he wholly followed the Lord God of Israel. And the name of Hebron formerly was Kirjath Arba (Arba was the greatest man among the Anakim). Then the land had rest from war. (Joshua 14:10-14)

The above decree came from an 85-year-old man. Along with Joshua, he was the only other surviving man from all those who left Egypt with

Moses. The two of them were granted this privilege because over 40 years ago, they were the only ones among a group of twelve spies who were confident God was going to give them the land that He promised and take it from all the giants.

Caleb knew what God had destined for Him, and he knew the mountain and government for his life. He didn't let time or what other people perceived of him corrupt his faith and prevent him from receiving God's promises for his life. Caleb and Joshua had the same mindset when it came to believing God, and those promises rejuvenated their physical bodies. Caleb said he was as strong at 85 as he was when he was in his 40s because his strength was for war, for going out and coming in.

Despite the cities of the giants being great and fortified, Caleb knew the God of war was with him and was on his side, and that God would enable him to drive out the giants. Joshua came into agreement with Caleb's decree and blessed him, then he gave Hebron to Caleb for his inheritance. Both Caleb and Joshua had future generations on their mind. Do you know that your government in the here and now will also affect your generation? How we steward our government will affect our generation, for good or bad.

So the scripture said, after Caleb decreed what was promised to him and Joshua blessed him and gave Hebron to Caleb, Hebron become Caleb's inheritance even before he physically drove out the giants. You and I coming into agreement with the government God has destined for us releases everything He has for us in the spirit realm, even before we possess it in the natural realm. The scriptures said Hebron became Caleb's inheritance because he followed God with all his might. He didn't go before God, instead he followed the Lord, knowing this would all happen according to God's timing, not his. Now look at verse 15. It says the name of Hebron was formerly named after Arba, the greatest man of the Anakim tribe of giants. But it now has a new name indicating it has a new landlord, Hebron belongs to Caleb and his generation (inheritance). An inheritance always has future generations in mind. A name represents the identity, character, function, influence, authority and government of a person, place or thing. This is important. Once the mountain and government over Hebron changed from the giants (Arba) to the rightful owner in the spirit, the result was that the specific, natural territory (land) which was under the new government of the mountain, had rest from war. Caleb's mountain (government) released peace over the land.

Later in our journey in this book we will discuss how we are called to function in our individual mountain (government).

DISCUSSION POINTS:

What does a mountain represent?

Why did the Giants reside on the mountains?

What did the high places represent?

On what part of the mountain was the altar and seat of authority positioned?

Why did God have the righteous kings destroy the high places in Israel?

What did Caleb do to enter his mountain (government)?

What were the results of Caleb entering his mountain (government) in the earth realm?

ENDNOTES:

https://www.nationalgeographic.com/science/earth/surface-of-the-earth/mountains/

https://en.wikipedia.org/wiki/Mount_Olympus

https://en.wikipedia.org/wiki/Book_of_Enoch

CHAPTER 2
THE ISAIAH COMPANY (THE MOUNTAIN-EAGLE INTERDEPENDENCE)

*But those who **wait** on the Lord Shall **renew their strength**; They shall mount up with wings like eagles, They shall run and not be weary, They shall walk and not faint.* (Isaiah 40:31)

In the Bible, the eagle represents strength, the prophetic which is connected to God's vision (eyesight). The prophet Isaiah was known as the Eagle Eye Prophet due to his accurate prophetic insights into the future. He prophesied accurately about Christ's birth, life, death, resurrection, and second coming over 700 years before it happened.

Later in this chapter we will discover the beautiful God given features of the eagle that cause it to stand out amongst all the other birds.

God is sending out a clarion, invitational call to all who desire to walk with Him in a very special and intimate way; who yearn to walk on the ancient paths, the paths less trodden by man; the ones only trodden by God and those who want Him more than anything else (see Proverbs 8). Because the eagle sees from a different PERSPECTIVE, I believe in this era and season God is raising up a company of believers that He is calling the Isaiah Company. These individuals will be connected to the eagle by operating in the spirit the same way an eagle operates in the natural. They will also be connected to the mantle of Isaiah as the eagle eye prophetic; accurately discerning and seeing what God is currently doing and will do in the future as they ascend. In the past, a mantle was typically passed down to a single person, but I believe in this season mantels and assignments will be assigned to a company of believers; those who fit the "Whosoever is Hungry for it" label. It will be a company of like-minded men and women of God who will accept this open invitation from God. As we journey together in this book, we will share more about this special invitation. Let's go further in discovering more about this Eagle group, the Isaiah Company.

The Isaiah Company will have a perspective and vision that comes from third heaven engagement and intercession, similar to how the eagles dwell, and observe the skies, and land below from the mountain cliffs. This third heaven engagement function is another way the Isaiah Company relates to the prophet Isaiah.

In the year that King Uzziah died, I saw the Lord sitting on a throne, high and lifted up, and the train of His robe filled the temple. Above it stood seraphim; each one had six wings: with two he covered his face, with two he covered his feet, and with two he flew. And one cried to another and said: "Holy, holy, holy is the Lord of hosts; The whole earth is full of His glory!" And the posts of the door were shaken by the voice of him who cried out, and the house was filled with smoke. So I said: "Woe is me, for I am undone! Because I am a man of unclean lips, And I dwell in the midst of a people of unclean lips; For my eyes have seen the King, The Lord of hosts." Then one of the seraphim flew to me, having in his hand a live coal which he had taken with the tongs from the altar. And he touched my mouth with it, and said: "Behold, this has touched your lips; Your iniquity is taken away, And your sin purged." Also I heard the voice of the Lord, saying: "Whom shall I send, And who will go for Us?" Then I said, "Here am I! Send me." And He said, "Go... (Isaiah 6:1-9a)

Notice that this third heaven engagement started out with something profound,, "In the year that King Uzziah died, he saw the Lord sitting on 'His' throne, high and lifted up." In 2 Chronicles 26 you can read the scripture account of Uzziah's reign. In a short summation, he assumed the throne at 16, and as he followed the ways of the Lord, he prospered as

God gave him great success in resources and military victories. Because of these blessings, Uzziah's fame spread throughout the nations around him.

This fame was intended to ultimately bring glory to the God of Israel, but verse 16 says when he was strong (at the pinnacle of his reign), his heart became lifted up in pride. Just like anything else in our heart (our inner man) that develops internally, it will be revealed through our actions. In King Uzziah's case, his besetting sin was pride, which God hates. From verse 16 on, things drastically went downhill for King Uzziah. He allowed the spirit of pride to control him to the point that he refused to follow the path God had laid out for the nation of Israel. He also refused to yield to God's intended design and functions for kings and usurped functions that were reserved for the Levitical priesthood, which were the descendants of Aaron (Moses's brother).

> **SIDENOTE:** Thank God through Jesus Christ we are now part of the priesthood of Melchizedek, being kings and priests unto our God (see Genesis 14, Hebrews 5:6-10, Hebrews 6:13-20, Hebrews 7:1-21, and Revelation 1:1-2).

So back to King Uzziah. He allowed the spirit of pride to drive him to the point where he defied the commandments of God regarding the priestly duties and their exclusive functions in the temple. Uzziah went in and burned incense on the altar of incense, despite God designating that duty solely to the priesthood.

"This" king did not have the authority or permission from God to do that. Now keep in mind, King Uzziah was offering up incense, which can represent prayers or intercession out of a "spirit of pride." This led to an altercation as Azariah and 80 priests confronted the king. They were furious because they knew the magnitude of the king's intentional rebellion. They understood his transgression was not only against them, but most importantly, against God Himself. Notice in verse 18 that Azariah and the 80 priests were called valiant (men of courage and substance). These 81 men of valor told the king that he was not permitted to be there and to leave;

and that **"You *shall have* no honor from the Lord God."** This was profound, as the pronouncement struck right to the heart of the king's heart issue. The priests, functioning in their priestly role as intercessor between God and man, spoke God's heart to the king. In verse 19, it says when the king heard this, rather than repent his pride caused him to become furious. While he was holding the censer and continued to be angry with the priests, God struck him with leprosy, which was a symbolic disease of being unclean and unfit. God validated the priests BECAUSE of the spirit of pride the king allowed to envelop him.

Being a leper, the priests threw him out of the temple, and the king, now realizing that God had humbled him with leprosy due to his pride and disobedience, rushed out. Uzziah's remaining days consisted of him living as a leper, the lowest of the low in Israeli society. Due to the contagious nature of this disease, he was ostracized and lived in an isolated house, and the kingship was taken from him.

I wanted to include this background regarding King Uzziah because I believe that prophet Isaiah's third heaven engagement (seeing and hearing in the spirit) was contingent on King Uzziah's death, the death of the power of pride. If I could paraphrase Isaiah 6:1, it would say, "Once the power and authority of pride (King Uzziah) died, THEN my spiritual eyes were opened to see the Lord sitting on 'his' throne, high and lifted up."

Pride goes before destruction, And a haughty spirit before a fall. (Proverbs 16:18)

FALSE HUMILITY IS PRIDE GIFT WRAPPED IN RELIGION

True humility is simply believing what God said about you and walking in that God given identity. God places such a high value on our identity because it cost Jesus His life, and he has given us the seal of His inheritance, His Holy Spirit. We have received the blood of Jesus for our salvation, having been born again or re-made in His image and after His likeness. As Jesus IS (right now), so are we (right now) in this earth.

Love has been perfected among us in this: that we may have boldness in the Day of Judgment; **because as He is, so are we in this world.** (1 John 4:17)

So many times we need to take the layers of religious junk off and out of us; such as some of the mistaken things we have been led to believe; the things others have said over us; everything we thought about ourselves, which was and is way beneath how God sees us, and what He has said over us. Many times, if we don't have a healthy self-image of who we are (in Christ), when we hear and see what God really says about us and thinks toward us, in our natural and un-renewed mind, it can appear daunting and even unbelievable, unrealistic or unattainable. Many times, false humility will enable you to see what God says about someone else and accept it, while prohibiting yourself from having the same attitude for yourself to believe and envision what God has said, and is saying about you. And that is when the enemy effectively employs his weapon of false humility.

False humility is a demonic religious spirit that can lead you into believing anything, excluding what God has said about YOU. God made you to be an eagle. It's important to go up, as an eagle, to see for yourself what God has said about you and how He sees you. Once you know what God says about you, then you can start developing it in your imagination. Religion will have you say and repeat things in the Word without you really imagining or seeing yourself that way; therefore, there is no faith initiating your words. If we don't use the Word of God to "build and develop" that image in us, then repeating what God says about us is nothing more than religious jargon with no power to change us, because faith is not connected to it.

Only after Isaiah ascended into the third heaven engagement, seeing, hearing, and engaging with God's love, holiness, glory, and the seraphim around the throne, and only then was his true identity made known. Seeing God **caused** Isaiah to truly see himself in his current condition. Isaiah saw who he was supposed to be, based on his interaction with God his creator. **Then,** Isaiah judged himself and came to the conclusion that he just didn't measure up.

So I said: "Woe is me, for I am undone! Because I am a man of unclean lips, And I dwell in the midst of a people of unclean lips; For my eyes have seen the King, The Lord of hosts." (Isaiah 6:5)

But the good news is, although this may have caught Isaiah by surprise, it didn't catch God or Heaven (the Seraph) off guard. God had already made provisions for Isaiah. Once the power of pride (King Uzziah) died and Isaiah saw God and his identity in God, he humbly confessed that he didn't measure up. The spirit of humility Isaiah displayed was the open door or permission God needed to allow the Seraph to minister to Isaiah with a live coal from heaven's altar. That is reassuring for me and it should be for you as well, that our past failures and current condition of becoming more like Christ doesn't cut us off from God using us as we continue humbling ourselves under his loving hand.

Therefore humble yourselves under the mighty hand of God, that He may exalt you in due time, casting all your care upon Him, for He cares for you. (1 Peter 5:6-7)

RELATIONSHIP FIRST, THEN FUNCTION

It has always been God's design for creation to be relational first and then functional. That is His own nature and how he chooses to interact with His most prized creation...man. As it did with Isaiah, our relationship and fellowship with God reveals our identity, and out of that true identity our true function in the earth will come forth. We see throughout scriptures how certain individuals were given their God given name before they were born; giving them an advantage in fulfilling God's destiny in the earth, such as Jesus and John the Baptist, due to their purpose being the actual meaning of their name. Also in the bible, people's names were sometimes changed after a powerful encounter with God. Names represent identity, character, purpose, and destiny. For those who were on the wrong path or not on their God ordained path, this name change represented a new direction in their life. Some people whose names were changed are Abraham, Peter, Israel (Jacob), and Benjamin, to name a few. Once their names were changed, their lives (functions) also dramatically changed for the better. I don't know about you, but I consider that GOOD news because I was born into sin and shaped in iniquity (Psalm 51). So the enemy, Satan our accuser, was often stating facts in his accusations against me and you (Revelation 12:10). But thank God for His grace, and for that grace giving us an opportunity to receive the power of Christ's blood. Praise God that Jesus made provisions for us through His blood, and has given us access to heavenly places in Him!

We see in verse 4 of Isaiah 6 that the frequency and glory that was on God's voice shook what I like to call the "access door." This access door is important for the Isaiah Company. We see a reference to this door in the book of Revelation:

*After these things I looked, and behold, a **door standing open** in heaven. And the first voice which I heard was like a trumpet speaking with me, saying, "Come up here, and I will show you things which must take place after this."* (Revelation 4:1)

Notice it says the access door is standing open. And guess what? It is still open for those of us who are in Christ.

Jesus said to him, "I am the way, the truth, and the life. No one comes to the Father except through Me." (John 14:6)

I am the door. If anyone enters by Me, he will be saved, and will go in and out and find pasture. (John 10:9)

*This hope we have as an anchor of the soul, both sure and steadfast, and which enters the Presence behind the veil, where **the forerunner** has entered for us, even Jesus, having become High Priest forever according to the order of Melchizedek.* (Hebrews 6:19-20)

So we see that Christ is the way, the ancient path, and the access door. He has also entered in the Holy of Holies behind the veil, as our Forerunner.

The spirit of pride is a cunning spirit and mindset that will lift everything else up, except for God and the things of God. Regarding King Uzziah in the temple, someone on the outside may say, "I don't see the big deal with what he did in the temple." You could say that he was trying to do a good thing in offering incense to God. If anyone thinks that, I would like to state that if the intention of your heart is corrupt, then the action stemming from it is also corrupt. This impure motive will lead you on a path contrary to God's heart and mind, as was in the case of lucifer (Ezekiel 28:14-17, Absalom (2 Samuel 14-18), and also King Uzziah, just to name a few.

So as the Isaiah Company, we must intentionally ask God to reveal to us anything in our soul that needs to be dealt with. God is so loving and gracious, and when we ask with an intentional heart desiring to please Him, He will lovingly show us what is there and what needs to be done. That mindset toward the Lord will continually put us in a position where we can be transformed and go up to see from an eagle's perspective, as the Isaiah Company is destined.

*[Then] He will cover you with **His pinions, and under His wings** shall you trust and find refuge; His truth and His faithfulness are a shield and a buckler.* (Psalm 91:4 AMPC)

In the Gospels, we see that Jesus lived as the perfect example of the Isaiah Company. His engagement with the Father allowed Him to live from an eagle's perspective. He would continually go UP into the Mountain to pray, engage the Father, receive from Heaven, and then bring what He received from the Father down to the earth to release it into the earthly realm.

The eagles' perspectives of the Isaiah Company are connected with Heaven and God's AERIAL viewpoint. The natural eagle sees things from a totally different viewpoint than man and land animals, such as a dog, a cat, or even a giraffe, the tallest animal that currently walks the earth.

The vertical and aerial level (heavenly view) will always supersede the horizontal and ground level (earthly view).

"Thus says the Lord of hosts: 'If you will walk in My ways, And if you will keep My command, Then you shall also judge My house, And likewise have charge of My courts; I will give you places to walk Among these who stand here. (Zechariah 3:7)

I believe the Lord is revealing to the Isaiah Company the three levels of the third heaven intercession released in Zechariah 3:7:

1) First Level: Judge my house (as a righteous king) as Christ is King of all kings and Lord of all lords.
2) Second Level: Have charge of my heavenly courts.
3) Third Level: Given places to walk among those who stand here (in heavenly places).

TERRESTRIAL LEVEL (EARTHBOUND)

There are a few species of birds, such as chickens that only fly very low to the ground. These types of birds will be considered terrestrial or earth bound because their vision and experience is limited to the earth. The chicken does not see from heaven's perspective, or from a throne room perspective like the eagle, because the chicken's perspective is based off an earth level viewpoint. Chickens and birds who live and fly on the terrestrial level have to be continually on guard and conscious of their surroundings to avoid all the predators on the land like them, and those predators who are above them.

Praying at the terrestrial level: First, I want to share that God is with us and He promised to never leave us nor forsake us. So we can always take comfort and encouragement in that. Praying at this level and on this level can put you at a disadvantage when it comes to spiritual warfare against the enemy. Unless you have an idea and scope of the domain and terrain that may have been taken from above. Battling from a horizontal level will increase your odds of receiving severe damage or become a casualty of war.

TREETOP LEVEL (HEAVENLY REALMS)

There are species of birds that fly higher than chickens, but lower than most other birds. These birds fly slightly above the trees but well below the clouds. Many times you see them congregating together on electrical lines. These birds have a slightly higher perspective than just the earthly, terrestrial view (chickens). I call this view the treetop view. While this treetop view is higher than the chickens' earthly view, the birds on this level are confronted with a lot of turbulence, contrary winds, harsh weather, birds of prey, and other birds that challenge them to defend or invade territory. I would also equate this treetop level as heavenly places. There is a difference between heavenly places in Christ and just heavenly places. Heavenly places are spiritual places and domains either evil or godly spirits can occupy. Similar to the treetop level with its many birds, some of those treetop level birds are no threat to other birds. Other birds at this level can lead to the death of birds who live in the treetop space.

Scriptures referencing heavenly places: For we do not wrestle against flesh and blood, but against principalities, against powers, against the rulers of the darkness of this age, against spiritual hosts of wickedness in the heavenly places. (Ephesians 6:12)

To the intent that now the manifold wisdom of God might be made known by the church to the principalities and powers in the heavenly places. (Ephesians 3:10)

There is rarely any protection from storms on the treetop level. The birds on this level have to react because they most likely didn't see or discern the coming storms from their position.

Praying at the treetop level: Praying from this level provides you a better advantage than praying at the ground horizontal level. The treetop level also exposes you to many animals lurking in the trees ready to pounce, or other birds that can be detrimental to you. Also, praying at this level, spiritually, tends to thwart and corrupt your view of things that are below, due to all of the voices, sounds, and activities taking place on the treetop level. Also, praying from this level can produce fear-based prayers.

It can be very difficult and challenging to distinguish God's voice amongst all the distractions on this level. The treetop level provides a higher view and perspective than the terrestrial view; yet, the treetop level is not God's best design of prayer for us. There is a higher calling and invitation that God is offering us, and that is to dwell and pray from the mountain level.

MOUNTAIN LEVEL (THRONE ROOM)

Then there is the eagle, which has the mountain and cloud level viewpoint and perspective. Many eagles live and build their nests in the cliffs of the mountains. This area is a secret place because not many enemies have access to this high mountainous region; the only viable threat to the eagle is man, and that's only if the eagle leaves the secret place, the mountain. So the only thing that can REALLY stop you is YOU, your mindset, your limitations in your mind.

Now to Him who is able to do exceedingly abundantly above all that we ask or think, according to the power that works in us. (Ephesians 3:20)

There, in the high places (the cliffs of the mountains), the eagles can raise their young to the point of maturity where they can survive on their own. I also call this the mountain level, the throne room perspective for the Isaiah Company. This is what the Bible would call the heavenly places in Christ. Through persistence and abiding in God in the heavenly places in Christ, this engagement can quickly shift into throne room intercession, where we get God's heart and God's viewpoint regarding particular matters in the earth. This is where He shares his secrets with us because we are in the secret place with Him.

The secret [of the sweet, satisfying companionship] of the Lord have they who fear (revere and worship) Him, and He will show them His covenant and reveal to them its [deep, inner] meaning. (Psalm 25:14 AMPC)

The mountain level where the eagle dwells alone can be compared to the heavenly places IN CHRIST. There is a level and domain in Christ that the enemy cannot access, nor do they want to, because it's located in Christ

(The Anointed One and His Anointing). The evil spirits and principalities want no part of the activated glory that resides within us because we are IN Christ. Acts 17:28 says that in Him (Christ) we live, move, and have our being (Identity).

Scriptures of…in the Heavenly Places **in Christ**: *Blessed be the God and Father of our Lord Jesus Christ, who has blessed us with every spiritual blessing in the heavenly places in Christ...* (Ephesians 1:3)

And raised us up together, and made us sit together in the heavenly places in Christ Jesus… (Ephesians 2:6)

Praying at the mountain level: At this level there are no distractions because the enemy doesn't have access to this level (Heavenly places in Christ). You can easily discern what God is showing you and saying to you, similar to the prophet Isaiah in Isaiah 6. Also, since we can clearly see and hear what God is saying about the situation below, we can capture God's heart and mind regarding those situations, and our prayers then become decrees (authoritative prayers). Our decrees from this realm consist of repeating what God has already said in the heavenlies, and we repeat it in the heavenlies AND on earth in agreement. We repeat it in the heavenlies for the principalities and evil forces who dwell in that domain to hear, and we repeat it in the earthly realm for the lower rank evil forces to hear. And we repeat it for man (humanity), and creation who is subject to the Word of God to hear, and for God's angelic realm who heed to the Word.

ACTIVATION:

Does the eagle mount up at your command, And make its nest on high? On the rock it dwells and resides, On the crag of the rock and the stronghold. From there it spies out the prey; Its eyes observe from afar. (Job 39:27-29 ESV)

In this activation, I want you to see yourself as an eagle flying up as God calls you to your mountain. As you fly around your mountain, you look down and see the top of the trees way down below. You also look even further below toward the ground, observing all the hustle and bustle on the ground level. You see it all from your mountain view. As you are looking, you lock your wings and allow yourself to rest on the winds as you soar effortlessly in the spirit. Even while typing this activation out, I was engaging and saw my angel and other angels of the Lord being drawn to me, flying beside me in the heavenlies. I want you to write down and document in your journal the things you observe in this engagement.

You will also declare a thing, And it will be established for you; So light will shine on your ways. (Job 28:22)

There are fewer birds and other animals at this high level for a variety of reasons, such as the high altitude, the air quality and oxygen level, temperature, and mountainous terrain. At times, dwelling in the mountains can be a lonely place, but thank God we have a God who communes with us in a very special way. Living intimately with God at this level makes it worth the cost.

THE STORM

I read that an eagle can "discern" when a storm is approaching long before it arrives. The eagle will then fly to some high location like a mountain's cliff and wait for the winds to come. When the storm hits, the eagle sets and spreads its wings so the wind will pick him up and lift him above the storm. While the storm rages below, ravaging all those caught in its path, the eagle is effortlessly soaring above it, resting its wings. The eagle does not escape the storm. It simply uses the wind created by the storm to lift it to a higher level, even before the full measure of the storm is unleashed. This is the benefit of discerning the storm from afar. And this is also a type of operating in authority above the storm as we live in heavenly places in Christ during the storm.

Earthbound birds AND treetop birds will most likely be unsettled, anxious, and uncomfortable because of the storm that is "upon" them, because they are exposed to its elements and subjected to whatever the storm releases onto the trees and terrain below the storm. The birds on this level will have to **react** to the storm's fury.

FEATURES THAT MAKE THE EAGLE STAND OUT

As we read earlier, the Isaiah Company is compared to Eagles. Below are some interesting qualities of eagles that are also a benefit to the function of the Isaiah Company in the spirit realm.

EAGLE'S VISION:

The eagle's vision is extremely powerful and considered to be one of the most powerful in the animal kingdom; it is estimated to be 4-8 times better than the average human. An eagle can visually spot a rabbit around 3.2 km away, which is almost two miles!! So an eagle's perspective (Throne Room perspective) will provide a whole different outlook on something on the earth, compared to an earthly (terrestrial) or treetop perspective.

Eagles have eyelids that close while they sleep. For blinking, they **have** an inner **eyelid** called a nictitating membrane. Every three or four seconds, the nictitating membrane slides across the eye from front to back, wiping dirt and dust from the cornea. In Job 31:1, Job said he made a covenant with his eyes; he understood the importance and responsibility we have to guard our spirit man through our sight gate, keeping our spiritual eyes clean from the dirt and dust the enemy attempts to use to pollute our vision.

> SIDENOTE: God has enabled the Isaiah Company and all of His Children the ability to see in the spirit realm with our spiritual eyes that are connected to our born again inner man.

And Elisha prayed, "Open his eyes, Lord, so that he may see." Then the Lord opened the servant's eyes, and he looked and saw the hills full of horses and chariots of fire all around Elisha. (2 Kings 6:17)

Being predatory birds, an **Eagle's eyes** are located towards the front of their head. However, their **eyes** are angled 30 degrees away from the midline of the face, giving them a 340-degree field of **vision**.

SIDENOTE: One of the main foods eagles enjoy eating are serpents, and many times they use their talons (sharp and long claws) and beak to kill the snake. So they use the two main things God has given the Isaiah Company to use. He has created our feet to tread on serpents with the feet of the gospel of peace. And he has given us our mouth, which we are admonished to speak out the Word of God with faith.

Behold, I give unto you power to tread on serpents and scorpions, and over all the power of the enemy: and nothing shall by any means hurt you. (Luke 10:19 KJV)

And having shod your feet with the preparation of the gospel of peace... (Ephesians 6:15)

And take the helmet of salvation, and the sword of the Spirit, which is the word of God... (Ephesians 6:17)

The **eagle can look directly** into the **sun**. The sight of the eagle is very sharp and it can see fish swimming when flying over water. Young eagles cannot locate fish below water as a result of a refraction error of their eye, so they compensate by grabbing dead fish floating on the surface. As they grow older and mature, the refraction error rectifies itself, enabling them to spot fish below the surface of the water.

"While we do not look at the things which are seen, but at the things which are not seen. For the things which are seen are temporary, but the things which are not seen are eternal." (2 Corinthians 4:18 NKJV)

SIDENOTE: Similar to a person going to the gym to build muscles through working out, so it is in the spirit. As we practice the things of God in the spirit, our discernment will also increase and sharpen so we can see the thing (spiritually) behind the thing (naturally). Godly discernment will enable us to righteously judge the intent of a person, place or thing; and this includes the human spirit, the demonic or heavenly spirits sent by the Lord.

But solid food belongs to those who are of full age, that is, those who by reason of use have their senses exercised to discern both good and evil. (Hebrews 5:14)

The **Eagle's** eyesight makes him an expert hunter...**Eagles**, like all birds, have excellent **color** vision. They **see colors** more vividly than we **do** and **can** distinguish more shades. They also **see** ultraviolet light, enabling them to detect the urine trails of small prey.

It is noted that pound for pound, an eagle's wing is stronger than the wing of an airplane. Most eagles have wings that are rather long and wide to help them soar and glide with less effort. The Eagles (the Isaiah Company) will fly and soar with God's grace, moving through heavenly places in Christ.

I am the door. If anyone enters by Me, he will be saved, and will go in and out and find pasture. (John 10:9)

Eagles fly alone at a high altitude, and **do** not mix with sparrows or **other** smaller **birds** like geese. **Birds** of a feather flock together. No **other** bird ascends to the height of the **eagle**. No matter the obstacle, the **eagle** will not remove his focus from the prey until he grabs it.

> SIDENOTE: When it comes to functioning in our identity, eagles do not mix with other birds. This is not talking about interacting with the unsaved for relationship toward salvation as Jesus did in the Gospels.

The acceleration of an eagle is unmatched. From its perch atop high trees or mountains, the eagle can dive at speeds of 125–200 miles per hour (201–322 km/h) to catch its prey with its talons.

Also notice that Golden eagles are mostly silent, except during the breeding season! This is very noteworthy, Golden eagles release a frequency when it's time to produce after their own kind. Unlike many other animal species, Golden eagles don't use vocalizations to mark their territory. Instead, they mark the edges of their territory by flying around them.

MATURITY (THE THREE P'S OF THE EAGLE)

Like an eagle that stirs up its nest, that flutters over its young, spreading out its wings, catching them, bearing them on its pinions... (Deuteronomy 32:11 ESV)

Mature Eagles are PURPOSEFUL, exemplifying PERSISTENCE and PATIENCE in helping their eaglets (baby eagles) develop to maturity. After the chicks hatch out of the egg, the eaglet goes through a fledging process where the young bird will develop wing feathers that are large enough for flight, which usually takes place around 10 weeks of age. The golden eagle attains its full skeletal size in 8-10 weeks

BE AND VEX THE ENEMY

As the Isaiah Company, we are to speak and decree God's Word out of our mouths. But there will be times, as we walk and fly in our identity in Christ (our state of BEing), that our mere presence will send the enemy into a panic fit!

Now in the synagogue, there was a man who had a spirit of an unclean demon. And he cried out with a loud voice, saying, "Let us alone! What have we to do with You, Jesus of Nazareth? Did You come to destroy us? I know who You are—the Holy One of God!" But Jesus rebuked him, saying, "Be quiet, and come out of him!" And when the demon had thrown him in their midst, it came out of him and did not hurt him. Then they were all amazed and spoke among themselves, saying, "What a word this is! For with authority and power He commands the unclean spirits, and they come out." (Luke 4:33-36)

You see how Jesus was just being who He was (living in His state of Being) and the demon was vexed by Jesus being in close proximity? I believe this is the place where God will have the Isaiah Company walking in a deeper way. The enemy will expose himself...Praise God!

SIDENOTE: You were created to be a wild eagle, but religion desires you to be a domesticated bird.

DOMESTICATED BIRDS VS. WILD EAGLES

Birds were originally created to fly. There is a creative design for birds possessing wings. I will use chickens in this example. As many chickens have become more domesticated in captivity, they are less inclined to fly away than other birds who are in the wild. When some domesticated birds attempt to fly away because of panic or fear, they flap their wings passionately and excessively, while **at times running**. They may slightly elevate and get their feet off the ground but depending on their breed they may not be able to fly higher than a short fence. There are even many domesticated chickens whose wings are clipped intentionally to keep them **contained** and grounded. This prevents them from utilizing their wings in the way they were created, **to ascend**. Captivity causes even the life of an eagle to change significantly in its quality. Yes, the lifespan of an eagle in captivity may increase because many of its predators are removed, and the domesticated eagle doesn't risk eating any type of poison or toxins. But in the wild and natural habitat, the eagle is free to be the way God created it. If a fully mature eagle from the wild is captured and put into a cage, this can lead to major complications such as the eagle desiring to escape due to stress, or attempting to kill any small animal close by. It can lead to the animal being intensely aggravated and even depressed. Also, depending on the size of the cage, the eagle can lose its ability to fly. It can become so domesticated that its natural hunting skills atrophy and gradually decline in effectiveness, giving it a huge disadvantage if it was ever released back into the wild without being RE-trained how to survive. The domestication or captivity of a bird intended to be wild, such as an eagle, can be compared to the spirit of religion and tradition. As a son and daughter of God, the spirit of religion and tradition will limit your full potential and attempt to place you in bondage to legalism. It will have control over you, causing you to function and operate in a totally different way than what God created you to be. The spirit of religion's agenda is to create you in **its** image and likeness, instead of in God's unique image and likeness. The Golden eagle's wingspan can range between 5.9 to 7.5 feet. An animal with that wingspan was not created to be contained in a small cage that prevents the eagle from being able to spread its wings, let alone fly. The spirit of religion and tradition is an enemy to the Isaiah Company...the eagles.

The opposite of a man-made traditional and religious mindset is intimacy with God. Intimacy with the Lord will root out and suffocate the spirit of religion.

Ascending to God and engaging Him is a by-product of our intimate relationship with the Lord.

Let's see in the Word where God invites us to come up (ascend):

- Come up higher (Revelation 4:1)
- Come boldly before his throne (Hebrews 4:16)
- We have entered mount Zion (Hebrews 12:22)

SOME ACCOUNTS OF MAN ENGAG-
ING GOD IN INTIMACY:

- Adam in the Garden (Genesis 2)
- Enoch (Hebrews 11:5)
- Abraham (Genesis 17:1)
- Jacob saw God (Genesis 28:10-17)
- Jacob (Genesis 32:30)
- Moses (Exodus 24:1, 12-13)
- Moses and the 70 elders go to heaven and eat with God (Genesis 24:9-11)
- Isaiah (Isaiah 6)
- John the apostle (Revelation 1, 4)
- Paul the apostle (2 Corinthians 12:1-4)

EMBRACING THE UNIQUENESS OF THE EAGLE

- When God extends an open invitation to something new (renewed), special, and intimate, only a few accept the call. The same applies with the Isaiah Company: Just as Golden eagle sightings are rare in certain areas, the Isaiah Company will be a remnant of believers who will go against the common grain and ascend in communing with God. This will mean there may be times where you may feel you are alone.

- The natural mind (the flesh) will try to convince and persuade you to be average and not pursue the deeper things of God; it will try to talk you out of your place of being an eagle and dwelling in the mountains.

- Keep in mind that, just like lions are kingly animals on the land, the eagles are majestic birds in the air.

- As the Isaiah Company, we are not to be proud or arrogant eagles, but be bold in who we are in Christ and confident in where God has placed us in Him.

- As eagles (mountain level birds), we shouldn't be condescending toward treetop or terrestrial level birds that may have a different mindset than us, or who may not fly as high as us or other eagles in certain areas. At the same time, we should not be envious of other birds that may currently fly and soar higher than us. We may be at different levels, but we are still one family in Christ.

DISCUSSION POINTS:

What similarities does the Isaiah Company share with eagles?

What spirit did King Uzziah allow to control him?

Why was the death of King Uzziah so significant to the prophet Isaiah's Third Heaven engagement?

What is False Humility?

What does the term "Relationship First, Then Function" mean?

What are the differences between praying and engaging from the Terrestrial level vs. the Treetop level vs the Mountain level?

You were created to be a wild eagle, but _____ desires you to be a domesticated bird.

How does a domesticated bird differ from a wild eagle?

Do you see yourself more as a domesticated bird or as a wild eagle? What areas do you feel the Holy Spirit is challenging you to be a wild eagle in Him?

Endnote:

Eagle Vision article: https://en.m.wikipedia.org/wiki/Eagle_eye

https://www.google.com/search?source=hp&ei=0j1UXMuyG47l5gKo-q62QBw&q=eagles+vision&btnK=Google+Search&oq=eagles+vi-sion&gs_l=psy-ab.3..0l9.561.2862..3185...0.0..0.86.1106.14......0....1..gws-wiz.....0..35i39j0i131j0i67.945inJ5UdAA

Reference: Kochert, M., K. Steenhof, C. McIntyre, E. Craig. 2002. Golden Eagle (Aquila chrysaetos). Pp. 1-44 in A Poole, F Gill, eds. *The Birds of North America*, Vol. 684. Philadelphia: The Birds of North America.

CHAPTER 3

CONVERGENCE OF THE FOUR
FACE GOVERNMENT

Then I looked, and behold, a whirlwind was coming out of the north, a great cloud with raging fire engulfing itself; and brightness was all around it and radiating out of its midst like the color of amber, out of the midst of the fire. Also from within it came the likeness of four living creatures. And this was their appearance: they had the likeness of a man. Each one had four faces, and each one had four wings. Their legs were straight, and the soles of their feet were like the soles of calves' feet. They sparkled like the color of burnished bronze. The hands of a man were under their wings on their four sides; and each of the four had faces and wings. Their wings touched one another. The creatures did not turn when they went, but each one went straight forward. As for the likeness of their faces, each had the face of a man; each of the four had the face of a lion on the right side, each of the four had the face of an ox on the left side, and each of the four had the face of an eagle. Thus were their faces. Their wings stretched upward; two wings of each one touched one another, and two covered their bodies. And each one went straight forward; they went wherever the spirit wanted to go, and they did not turn when they went. (Ezekiel 1:4-12)

As for their rims, they were so high they were awesome; and their rims were full of eyes, all around the four of them. When the living creatures went, the wheels went beside them; and when the living creatures were lifted up from the earth, the wheels were lifted up. (Ezekiel 1:18-19)

Before the throne there was a sea of glass, like crystal. And in the midst of the throne, and around the throne, were four living creatures full of eyes in front and in back. The first living creature was like a lion, the second living creature like a calf, the third living creature had a face like a man, and the fourth living creature was like a flying eagle. The four living creatures, each having six wings, were full of eyes around and within. And they do not rest day or night, saying: "Holy, holy, holy, Lord God Almighty, Who was and is and is to come!" (Revelation 4:6-8)

The above passage shows us two different scriptural encounters with the Cherubim. God is so expansive in everything He does, and that includes the entirety of His creation. Let's consider the incredible diversity represented within the animal kingdom. We have the Paedophryne amanuensis, a newly discovered frog that doesn't even have a common name yet. It measures a scant .3 inches while the Blue Whale tops out at 198 tons and a length of around 100 feet. There is also huge variety including fish that fly, birds who can't fly, meat eaters, plant eaters, and they can be found in every climate and place from the extreme pressures of the depths of the sea several miles down to the highest altitudes, from the hottest desert to the coldest valleys. The same is found when we examine the plant kingdom. Look at the various trees, their shapes, the fruit that grows on some of them, the other vegetation on the earth, including the variety of different colors of flowers. When it comes to God's greatest creation, man, as described in Psalm 8, we see the pattern continuing. Consider all the different races in humanity, all bearing beautiful and distinct features.

God is so awesome. This creativity of God also applies to the angelic realm. The Bible only gives us a small glimpse into the angelic realm along with precious few descriptions of some of the heavenly beings that interacted with man. Just as we are continuously discovering new species, I believe there are many more tribes of heavenly beings that God has created for His pleasure and to even minister for us that he has chosen in his infinite wisdom to hide from us for the time being, knowing their look and uniqueness would blow our minds if we were to see them in their natural state. The two accounts of the Cherubim in Ezekiel and Revelation have many similarities, but there are also some key differences. On common element in both passages is that both groups of Cherubim are connected to the face of a Lion, Ox, Eagle and Man.

At this time, we will focus on Ezekiel's account in. Each of the four faces of the cherub in Ezekiel 1 carry an unique expression of God, representing a different aspect of Kingdom government that will assist us in reaching maturity in Christ, which will in turn lead us to fulfilling the Government of Christ on the earth.

Prior to Christ coming to the earth in the flesh, the scriptures have periodically shown different aspects of the four faces, government or anointings, on various individuals for certain times and for certain tasks and functions. But when Christ came, there was a merging and convergence of these four expressions and governments (four faces) in Christ.

While the governments and anointings of the four faces are still distinctively different from each other, their unique function is now able to operate in and through one man, Christ Jesus. This is what leads to convergence. Convergence is the movement of two or more independent things as they merge together toward a union. In this case, the convergence would involve the four faces of the cherub (The Lion, the Ox, the Eagle and the Man). The synergy comes from the benefits as the result of this convergence of the four faces, government, and anointings, such as the maturity of the manifested children of God: The same children of God that creation is currently groaning over and waiting for our manifestation. God is determined that we, the church, will be His reflection of heaven on the earths so that Jesus will get His inheritance:

I will declare the decree: The Lord has said to Me, "You are My Son, Today I have begotten You. Ask of Me, and I will give You The nations for Your inheritance, And the ends of the earth for Your possession." (Psalm 2:7-8)

NOW that WE ARE IN CHRIST and joint heirs with Him, we have been grafted in as adopted sons (males and females). As we mature in Christ as manifested Children of God in the earth, we are given the capacity and potential to walk in this convergent government, both as individuals and corporately as a company of people. This company has been called different names over the years: the Dove Company, the Enoch Company, the Joshua Generation, and the Benjamin Generation to name just a few; but the Lord has put it on my heart to call it the Isaiah Company, as discussed in the previous chapter. We see that the Eagle (the Prophetic and your Seer Nature Government) makes up ¼ of this government.

For whom He foreknew, He also predestined to be conformed to the image of His Son, that He might be the firstborn among many brethren. (Romans 8:29)

This passage tells us that Jesus is the firstborn of many brethren; or we could say Jesus is the first of His kind, or the first of a new creation, new species, or new breed.

The Cherubim were created by God for many wonderful purposes, just like all His creation. One of the main purposes of the Cherubs are to follow, protect and cover the glory of God. We see this reflected in the book of Ezekiel. The four Faces (Governments) of the Cherubim were also created to fully reflect the manifested children of God in the earth; which flows and operates with the seven spirits of God (see Isaiah 11:2-3, Revelation 1:4-5; 4:5). Yes, the Cherub (singular) was created before man. But God, in his infinite wisdom and knowing the end from the beginning, destined man, the sons of God, to be the most unique and vested beings under God. Psalm 8:5 says *"For thou hast made him (man) a little lower than the angels."* The original translation is *a little lower than God).* Those of us who have trusted in Christ and his finished work on Calvary are in God's family; we carry his DNA and nature inside of us, a benefit of the New Birth.

Yet death reigned from Adam to Moses, even over those whose sinning was not like the transgression of Adam, who was a type of the one who was to come. (Romans 5:14 ESV)

The first Adam, in the book of Genesis, was physically created before the last Adam (Jesus Christ), but the first Adam was made in the likeness of the last Adam (Jesus Christ). In other words, Jesus Christ was the blueprint (the designed plan, model, and representation of something or someone) that God followed when He formed Adam. Let me put it like this: While God was forming Adam, He had Jesus Christ His Son on His mind as the original. The man, Christ Jesus, was in the bosom of the Father before the foundation or creation of the world (see John 17).

As He is, so are we in this present world. This is why he proclaimed greater works will we do. Is that before the cross, after the cross, or does it include both? What is Christ doing now? Where is he located and seated right now?

As He IS, so are we NOW. Jesus has eagle vision because he is the first and ultimate convergence of man. He is the firstborn of many brothers (children). The government and anointing of the Cherub's four faces converge into Christ, and we are in Christ.

There is what I will call the fivefold ministry; apostles that are connected to the fivefold ministry, but every believer is apostolic. Also, there is what I call fivefold ministry prophets who are connected to the fivefold ministry. But as sons and daughters of God, we are prophetic.

And He Himself gave some to be apostles, some prophets, some evangelists, and some pastors and teachers, for the equipping of the saints for the work of ministry, for the edifying of the body of Christ, till we all come to the unity of the faith and of the knowledge of the Son of God, to a perfect man, to the measure of the stature of the fullness of Christ;... (Ephesians 4:11-13)

Ephesians 4:11-13 reveals that God has given the local church body "specialists," some to be apostles, prophets, evangelists, pastors and teachers. These functions, or what many call offices, are given to equip the saints for the work of the ministry; to edify and build up the Body of Christ until we all come to the unity of the faith and knowledge of Jesus Christ, as a mature person. As we proceed to talk about the Eagle and Ox, I want you to keep in mind that the context of Ephesians 4:11-13 shows us not everyone is called to be a fivefold ministry apostle or a prophet. But, we all have the capacity to be apostolic and prophetic. It's important to keep this in mind as we delve further into this topic.

GOVERNMENT OF THE EAGLE:
(THE PROPHETIC AND YOUR SEER NATURE)

Surely the Lord God does nothing, Unless He reveals His secret to His servants the prophets. (A prophetic people) (Amos 3:7)

After these things I looked, and behold, a door standing open in heaven. And the first voice which I heard was like a trumpet speaking with me, saying, "Come up here, and I will show you things which must take place after this." (Revelation 4:1)

In the previous chapter, we read about the functions of an eagle and how majestic this wonderful animal is. In this chapter, we will go further by discussing the government and anointing that radiates from the eagle's face, and how it relates to us, the Isaiah Company, on the earth. The government of the Eagle's face is the Prophetic and your Seer Nature government.

Pursue love, and desire spiritual gifts, but especially that you may prophesy. (1 Corinthians 14:1)

(Formerly in Israel, when a man went to inquire of God, he spoke thus: "Come, let us go to the seer"; for he who is now called a prophet was formerly called a seer.) (1 Samuel 9:9)

Our seer nature is when we, through Christ, are able to see and interact in the Spirit using sight and other spiritual senses. This supernatural nature from our Heavenly Father at times can be activated from birth as part of a providential calling from God, while others in Christ can grow in their seer nature to engage in the spirit realm through passionate pursuit by developing their spiritual senses. The more we practice, the greater our potential to grow in our seer nature. This is done through the desire.

> SIDENOTE: Those things we desire, we will honor; and the things we truly honor, we will pursue.

*If you abide in Me, and My words abide in you, you will ask what **you desire**, and it shall be done for you.* (John 15:7)

Our seer nature is our heritage as children of God.

But solid food belongs to those who are of full age, that is, those who by reason of use have their senses exercised to discern both good and evil. (Hebrews 5:14)

As I stated before, I believe that through the Holy Spirit, the Lord has enabled all His children to have the capacity to be prophetic. Our Heavenly Father is prophetic, for He shares and reveals things to us before they happen. Jesus, in the gospels, was prophetic in His earthly ministry. I also believe that when we believe, repent and receive the blood of Jesus in our born again experience, God imparts His DNA into our reborn spirit man; making us visionary and prophetic, just like our Heavenly Daddy.

*...as His divine power has given to us all things that pertain to life and godliness, through the knowledge of Him who called us by glory and virtue, by which have been given to us exceedingly great and precious promises, that through these **you may be partakers of the divine nature**, having escaped the corruption that is in the world through lust.* (2 Peter 1:3-4)

Even in the natural, this majestic bird displays a prophetic insight into how it can discern a storm afar off, even before many animals on land (the terrestrial level) and "treetop level" birds have even a hint that a storm is coming. Remember, the heavenly insight from the mountain of God will trump earthly terrestrial insights every time. As in the natural, so it is in the spiritual. I believe the Lord can also share things with our spirit before something happens to help prepare us ahead of time, if he so desires. The eagle is free and lives uninhibited with no limitations.

As we, the eagles, ascend and operate in the prophetic and our seer nature, we will see what God sees, and hear what God says in the heavenly places in Christ.

The Love of God And The Spirit of Wisdom
Are The Thriving Forces Within The
Government of the Eagle (1 Corinthians 13)

ACTIVATION:

*Each of them had four faces and four wings. Their legs were straight and their feet were like a calf's hoof, and they gleamed like burnished bronze. Under their wings on their four sides were human hands. As for the faces and wings of the four of them, their wings touched one another; their faces did not turn when they moved, each went straight forward. As for the form of their faces, each had the face of a man; all four had the face of a lion on the right and the face of a bull (ox) on the left, and **all four had the face of an eagle.** Such were their faces. Their wings were spread out above; each had two touching another being, and two covering their bodies. And each went straight forward; wherever the spirit was about to go, they would go, without turning as they went.* (Ezekiel 1:6-12 NASB)

I want you to intentionally use the above scripture as a door and gateway when you engage in meditation and focus. This passage is full of illustrations, so use your sanctified imagination as if this encounter is unfolding right before you, or possibly right before you as Ezekiel stands beside you. The Word is alive. In Christ we live, move, and have our being (Acts 17:28), so in Christ there is no timeline restriction regarding engagement. Christ is in the past, the present, is in the future, and you are in Christ. So, picture yourself there. You may want to start at the beginning of Ezekiel 1. In this activation, I want you to specifically focus on the eagle's face. Look at the features, listen to the shriek and sounds emanating from the face of the eagle, then ask Holy Spirit to reveal the eagle's government and anointing that He desires for you to operate in as part of the eagles, the Isaiah Company. Journal what you see, hear, observe and feel.

GOVERNMENT OF MAN: PRIESTHOOD OF MAN (BETWEEN HEAVEN AND EARTH)

*But that you may know that **the Son of Man has authority on earth** to forgive sins—he said to the paralytic—* (Mark 2:10 ESV)

45

Did you know that, just like Jesus the Son of Man, the children of men have authority in the earth? If there was one body part the enemy wishes he had, it would be your belly button. Did you know that your belly button gives you authority in the earthly realm that the devil wishes he had? The belly button is the indication that we came into the earth through the womb of a woman, and the spirit of the enemy has no legal access to do what he wants in the earth, unless he works through a man.

God, in His sovereignty, has delegated legal authority to man, starting with Adam in the garden before the fall. Rather than take seriously the charge given him, Adam willingly gave that power to Satan in the garden, and this is why it became necessary for Jesus to come as God manifest in the flesh. He needed an earthly suit with a belly button. We have seen instances in the Bible where heavenly beings manifested in the earth realm while looking like men; but unless they were born through a woman, they don't have the same God-given delegated authority in the earth as a born again man.

Indeed, the Sovereign LORD never does anything until he reveals his plans to his servants the prophets. (Amos 3:7 NLT)

God says in Amos that He will not do anything in the earth until He first reveals his plans or secrets with His servants, the prophets (a company of prophetic people), or His friends. In other words, He will partner and confide with men who are in covenant with Him before He does anything in the earth. Friendship with God is a higher level of relationship than that of being just sons. Just because we are His children, it doesn't mean we are going to obey and do what He asks of us. The higher and more intimate level of our relationship with God is to be sons (His children) who also happen to be His friends. We have the story of the prodigal or lost son in Luke 15:11-32, as an example of a foolish son who decided to follow his own passions, over the desires of his good father. Jesus said in John 15:14, *"You are My friends if you do whatever I command you."* We have a perfect example of God confiding and even having a counseling session with a covenant man, Abraham, whom God called His friend (Isaiah 41:8).

*And the Lord said, "**Shall I hide from Abraham what I am doing**, since Abraham shall surely become a great and mighty nation, and all the nations of the earth shall be blessed in him? For I have known him, in order that he may command his children and his household after him, that they keep the way of the Lord, to do righteousness and justice, that the Lord may bring to Abraham what He has spoken to him." And the Lord said, "Because the outcry against Sodom and Gomorrah is great, and because their sin is very grave, I will go down now and see whether they have done altogether according to the outcry against it that has come to Me; and if not, I will know." Then the men turned away from there and went toward Sodom, **but Abraham still stood before the Lord. And Abraham came near and said**, "Would You also destroy the righteous with the wicked?* (Genesis 18:17-23)

In verses 17-21, we see God taking counsel with Himself regarding whether he should confide in Abraham what He planned to do in the earth regarding the wicked cites of Sodom and Gomorrah, and the other cities in the plain. Contrary to the thoughts of the world, and even in the church, God would rather bless man rather than bring judgement.

In verses 22-23, we see Abraham reverently approaching and standing before the council of the Lord as an intercessor. Abraham is a righteous man, standing before the Lord as a priest, on behalf of his nephew Lot, along with other people in these cities. In Genesis 18:22-33, we see Abraham and God conversing over how God will judge the city. Abraham respectfully talks to God as a friend and priest. We also see God carrying on a dialogue with Abraham until he eventually agrees to reduce the number of righteous people to spare the city. God began saying He would spare the city if a mere fifty righteous people were found there, to only requiring ten righteous to spare his judgment. Verse 33 below shows us how their conversation ended.

When the Lord had finished speaking with Abraham, he left, and Abraham returned home. (Genesis 18:33 NJKV)

So, we see the Lord leaving after He finished speaking with Abraham, His friend. At the end of the day, God is God and His sovereign desire will be accomplished in the earth no matter what anybody thinks or does. God also has allowed Himself to be in fellowship and friendship with sons and daughters who are in covenant with Him, to accomplish His will in the earth. Following their conversation, God walked away. Sadly, we are never told what God's response may have been had Abraham respectfully petitioned God one more time to spare the city for less than ten righteous people.

The government of the face of man is the part of God that shows His vulnerability as He expresses His desires to relate to man.

For we do not have a High Priest who cannot sympathize with our weaknesses, but was in all points tempted as we are, yet without sin. (Hebrews 4:15)

An unregenerate man who is not born again from above is not in the Kingdom of light, and therefore cannot see God. We who are born from above are His children, the children of Light; and we are the light of the world because we have our daddy's nature in us; for God is Light. Religion attempts to convince you to see yourself lower than what God and heaven sees you as, but only if you will allow that.

Paul admonishes us in Colossians 3:2 of the importance of setting our affections on things above, and not on the earth or things in the natural. Our affections (our mind, will, emotions, and imagination) are connected to the seat of our passions, which is the throne of our soulish man. Whatever we have affection for; a passion for it will follow. In fact, our passionate desire for something demonstrates the fondness we have for that thing. So, with a passionate desire, we are to set our affection on things above, and not on things of this earth, such as religion and traditions which are not God inspired.

The things above are from another realm, one higher than the realm of the natural. These things above also include how God sees you and what God has sang over you. Your flesh and unrenewed mind will be blown, preventing you from being able to accept it. This means the things above will be things we have not heard, seen, nor experienced yet; and we may not have a grid for it until we encounter it, receive it, and release it into the earth. 1 Corinthians 2:9-10 says, *"But as it is written: **"Eye has not seen, nor ear heard, Nor have entered into the heart of man** The things which God has prepared for those who love Him. **"But God has revealed them to us through His Spirit.** For the Spirit searches all things, yes, the deep things of God."*

*What is man that You take thought of him, And the son of man that You care for him? Yet **You have made him a little lower than God**, And You **crown him with glory and majesty!** You make **him to rule over the works of Your hands**; You have put all things under his feet...* (Psalm 8:4-6 NASB)

As we are being transformed into His image by the glory of the Lord, we will develop the capacity and authority to rule over ALL of God's creation; for He has put all things under our feet, because everything is under Christ's feet, and we are in Him. As stated before, this only applies to those who have been born again by the blood of Jesus, where our spirit man has been regenerated, recreated and reborn from above. When this occurs, God then places us in His family and in His classification, because we have His Divine Nature inside of us. When my sons and daughter were born, they became babies and young children, they were not on my level of maturity or my status in life yet. But they immediately became members of my family and class. As they grow and mature, more responsibility will be granted to them. This is how it is with us and our Heavenly Daddy (see Galatians 4).

The Love of God is the Thriving Force Within the Government of Man (1 Corinthians 13)

ACTIVATION:

Each of them had four faces and four wings. Their legs were straight and their feet were like a calf's hoof, and they gleamed like burnished bronze. Under their wings on their four sides were human hands. As for the faces and wings of the four of them, their wings touched one another; their faces did not turn when they moved, each went straight forward. As for the form of their faces, **each had the face of a man**; all four had the face of a lion on the right and the face of a bull (ox) on the left, and all four had the face of an eagle. Such were their faces. Their wings were spread out above; each had two touching another being, and two covering their bodies. And each went straight forward; wherever the spirit was about to go, they would go, without turning as they went. (Ezekiel 1:6-12 NASB)

I want you to view the above scripture as a door and gateway as you engage in meditation and focus. See yourself there, you may want to start at the beginning of Ezekiel 1. In this activation, I want you to specifically focus on the face of the man. Look at the features and facial expressions. Then ask Holy Spirit to reveal the government and anointing He desires you to walk in as a son or daughter of God in the earth, who has a belly button. Journal what you see, hear, observe and feel.

GOVERNMENT OF THE LION: KINGSHIP

However, in the first year of Cyrus king of Babylon, King Cyrus issued a decree to build this house of God. (Ezra 5:13)

"You will also decide and decree a thing, and it will be established for you; And the light [of God's favor] will shine upon your ways. (Job 22:28 AMP)

A decree is an official order, mandate or proclamation issued by a legal authority such as a king.

The lion, for the most part, has no enemies, other than man or other male lions seeking to acquire territory; the lion sits on top of the food chain. Despite this designation, lions are actually very social animals with their pride (group or family of lions). When it comes to the air, the eagle likewise does not have any enemies, other than other eagles. Eagles also sits on top of the food chain within their respective terrain.

Lions roar into the air to let the animals lodged above in the trees, birds flying in the air, and animals off in the distance, know that he is there.

> SIDENOTE: In explaining the Lion, I will use the masculine tense but the Lion and all four faces applies to male and female for there is no distinction between genders regarding how God desires you to be. So this applies to sons and daughters of God.

The lion also roars deeply toward the ground to allow his presence to reverberate throughout his surroundings.

His roar into the air is intended to reveal his location to those around him; and the authority conveyed by his roar reveals his desire to protect his territory and pride (family of lions) from other male lions who seek to come to kill off his sons and restart his own family (pride).

The thief does not come except to steal, and to kill, and to destroy. I have come that they may have life, and that they may have it more abundantly. (John 10:10)

His roar also proclaims to potential enemies that there is a lion present, and that he is willing and capable of backing up the fury behind his roar.

The roar of a lion can be heard from nearly five miles away! The powerful roar of a lion can be as loud as 114 decibels, which is as loud as a thunderclap and louder than a jet at take off!

And He has on His robe and on His thigh a name written: KING OF KINGS AND LORD OF LORDS. (Revelation 19:16)

Jesus Christ is the King of all kings and Lord of all lords; and He is the Lion out of the tribe of Judah.

Decreeing is us co-creating with God and establishing His will in the earth in the now. Prophesying is when we go into our future with God and come back into our now and then speak it; we then begin living out history from God's perspective. Remember, God knows the end from the beginning.

Remember the former things of old, For I am God, and there is no other; I am God, and there is none like Me, Declaring the end from the beginning, And from ancient times things that are not yet done,... (Isaiah 46:9-10)

As we decree God's word through the government and anointing of the Lion Face, we co-create and co-labor with God.

(as it is written, "I have made you a father of many nations") in the presence of Him whom he believed—God, who gives life to the dead and calls those things which do not exist as though they did;... (Romans 4:17)

As the children of God, we have the Spirit of Life inside of us. And just like our Heavenly Daddy, we can also call those things which do not exist as though they do, as we look through the spiritual eyes of faith within our sphere of influence.

Forever, O Lord, your word is firmly fixed in the heavens. (Psalm 119:89 ESV)

Now, we don't just create something out of thin air, like a pink elephant with yellow spots, five legs and two tails, without God already creating it "first." But, as the younger lions of THE Lion of Judah, the Lord Jesus Christ, we do speak and co-create in the earth based on what God has already spoken and created in the spirit realm.

*An oracle is on **the lips** of a king; **his mouth** does not sin in judgment. A just balance and scales are the Lord's; all the weights in the bag are his work. It is an abomination to kings to do evil, for **the throne** is established by **righteousness. Righteous lips** are the delight of a king, and he loves him who **speaks** what is right. A king's wrath is a messenger of death, and a wise man will appease it. In the light of a king's face there is life, and his favor is like the clouds that bring the spring rain.* (Proverbs 16:10-15 ESV)

As kings of the Kingdom, God endows us with great authority, which is always accompanied with great responsibility. The words that proceed out of our mouths are weighty, to the point that verse 10 tells us that an oracle is on the lips of a king. Other translations say a divine sentence. An oracle is defined as a person who was gifted to be a designated portal for a supernatural entity to speak through https://en.wikipedia.org/wiki/Oracle. In the realms of darkness demonic spirits would use an oracle as a medium to speak through, causing the people to believe it was the 'gods' speaking through them. Through the revealed word of God, we know this counterfeit practice is forbidden, and true oracles are those who yield to Holy Spirit so he can speak directly through.

So, the lips and words of a king are compared to that of an oracle, showing us the importance of the words that come forth from our hearts (our spirit man) and out of our mouths in our kingship. Verses 10-15 provides us with God's original intent in the function of a king, and how the Lord designed kings to operate. This doesn't negate the fact that there are kings who are not functioning in the way God originally designed them to function in, because we all are giving the precious gift of free will.

Verse 10 shows us that God's original intent is for us as kings to not sin in judgement as an oracle of God. In verses 11-12 God graciously reminds us about true justice and righteousness, and that the throne (the seat of authority) is established by righteousness, the things that are right in God's eyes, and it's not God's intent for kings to operate and rule from an evil, and unjust heart.

Verse 13 takes us back to righteous lips (words) and speaking those things that are right. That's why it's so important to have the mind of Christ, and to have His Spirit within our hearts continually to rely and depend on Holy Spirit to lead and guide us while transforming us. Take note in verse 14 where it says that a king's wrath is a messenger of death. It's a messenger of death because, most likely in wrath, the wrathful words spoken from the king will not be favorable for the person or persons to whom the wrath is directed toward. Therefore, if the king speaks a sentence of negative judgement or death, that is what will be executed because of the authority he embodies and because of the seat of authority he rules from (the throne).

I am using the 'he' pronoun due to the context of the scripture, but this applies for males and females in the kingdom of God because Christ has made us all kings and priests unto our God. Now, on the flip side, in verse 15 it says in the light of the king's face there is life. The light here refers to the brightness, favor and prosperity that radiates from the king's face, and there life will dwell because most likely the king in this scenario will speak and decree blessings and favor toward a person, and just like the negative judgement was executed, this judgement of goodness will also be executed. From these verses we see that as kings we have a choice and a vital role to play.

BLACK BOLT

I truly enjoy DC and Marvel superhero movies and cartoons. There is a character in the Marvel universe named Black Bolt. Black Bolt is a righteous king who rules over a race of special people known as Inhumans. Unlike other superheroes with cool and glamorous powers, his signature power is his voice. When he utters his mouth to speak, it triggers a massive disturbance in the form of a highly destructive shockwave capable of leveling a city.

Because of the extreme danger posed by this power, he must exercise great discipline and caution to never carry on a conversation or speak a word. To prevent this, he has undergone rigorous mental training to prevent himself from uttering a sound he does not plan to speak, even in his sleep. Black Bolt usually remains completely silent, speaking through sign language or a spokesperson.

Because Black Bolt values the people around him and those he rules over, he realizes the responsibility his voice carries and the deadly consequences if his authority is used incorrectly or unrighteously. A casual word misspoken will damage and destroy the very people he loves if he allows even a split second of carelessness. He is careful and considerate to not use his words against his enemies unless it's absolutely necessary. Even if he is angry from some evil his enemy did intentionally, he uses discipline and restraint in formulating a response.

Black Bolt is unable to speak blessings because every word he spoke, whether good or bad, would bring destruction. Although a fictional character, his restraint and awareness to realize the potential for great harm, and the discipline he developed, are definitely great truths we can learn.

IT IS UP TO US

Will we use our words to bless ourselves and those within our sphere of influence, seeing things as God sees and speaking what God has already spoken, or will we allow ourselves to be deceived and used by the enemy to speak curses to those things and people that God wants us to bless?

The Love of God Is The Thriving Force Within The Government Of The Lion (1 Corinthians 13)

ACTIVATION:

*Each of them had four faces and four wings. Their legs were straight and their feet were like a calf's hoof, and they gleamed like burnished bronze. Under their wings on their four sides were human hands. As for the faces and wings of the four of them, their wings touched one another; their faces did not turn when they moved, each went straight forward. As for the form of their faces, each had the face of a man; all four had **the face of a lion** on the right and the face of a bull (ox) on the left, and all four had the face of an eagle. Such were their faces. Their wings were spread out above; each had two touching another being, and two covering their bodies. And each went straight forward; wherever the spirit was about to go, they would go, without turning as they went.* (Ezekiel 1:6-12 NASB)

Continue to use the above scriptures as a door and gateway as you engage in meditation and focus. See yourself there. In this activation, I want you to specifically focus on the face of the lion. Look at the fierce, yet gentle features of the lion. Observe the love and majesty in His eyes, the sounds of His roar, the frequency of his deep purr, and how it affects you. Ask Holy Spirit to reveal the Lion's government to you, and how He desires you to operate in this kingly anointing as a lion. Journal what you see, hear, observe and feel.

GOVERNMENT OF THE OX: APOSTOLIC SERVANTHOOD

Come to Me, all you who labor and are heavy laden, and I will give you rest. Take My yoke upon you and learn from Me, for I am gentle and lowly in heart, and you will find rest for your souls. For My yoke is easy and My burden is light." (Matthew 11:28-20)

The ox is a reliable and durable animal. It plows the ground regardless of the properties of the soil; the soil could be hardened, rocky, soft and loose and still the ox will diligently perform his duties without complaining. Not everyone is called tofunction as a fivefold Apostle according to Ephesians 4:11-16, but we all are called to be apostolic, bringing Heaven to Earth as the sent ones within our sphere of influence or in our God-ordained mountain (the government God has entrusted to us). Like the natural ox, we the apostolic children of God are mandated to persevere in faith and patience whether the spiritual terrain is soft (open and receptive to the things of God) or hard (not receptive to the things of God).

The apostolic individual begins to implement heaven's strategies and culture into the earth. The prayer model that Jesus laid out in Matthew 6:9-13 is an apostolic prayer with an apostolic model and mandate:

In this manner, therefore, pray: Our Father in heaven, Hallowed be Your name **Your kingdom come.**

Your will be done On earth as it is in heaven. *Give us this day our daily bread And forgive us our debts,*

As we forgive our debtors And do not lead us into temptation, But deliver us from the evil one. For Yours is the kingdom and the power and the glory forever. Amen. (Matthew 6:9-13)

As ambassadors of heaven, gateways of heaven, and the household of God on earth, we all have a responsibility to release heaven, take territories, and be both the initiators and instigators of heavenly transformation on the earth as Holy Spirit leads us (see Genesis 28:10-17).

Below are a few people in the Bible who were apostolic in their lives.

ADAM:

Adam had an apostolic mandate and commission to spread Eden from the garden to the whole earth, and I believe from the earth to the cosmos (to release the Kingdom to the barren planets, black holes and dark matter to return them to God's original intent that they had before Satan's rebellion).

> SIDENOTE: All of creation is waiting for the revealing of the man-ifested children of God.

For we know that the whole creation groans and labors with birth pangs together until now. Not only that, but we also who have the firstfruits of the Spirit, even we ourselves groan within ourselves, eagerly waiting for the adop-tion, the redemption of our body. (Romans 8:22-23)

NOAH:

Noah was apostolic as he received the instructions and heavenly blue-prints to build something on the earth that never existed before (the ark) to prepare for something that never happened before (the flood). You can read the plans and instructions God gave to Noah regarding the ark in Genesis 6-7.

ABRAHAM:

Abraham was apostolic as the vessel God used to release the blessing through Abraham into his seed. His seed would be compared to the stars in the sky and the sand on the seashore; and through Abraham's seed, Jesus Christ would come into the earth to pay for the sins of all mankind (see Genesis 22:15-19).

MOSES:

Moses was apostolic because he received the blueprints from heaven on how to build the Tabernacle of Moses. He wasn't only given specific blueprints for the Tabernacle, but for the bronze laver, the altar of incense, the ark of the covenant, the table for the showbread, the gold lampstand, the altar of burnt offering, the court of the tabernacle, the garments for the priesthood, the ephod, the breastplate for the high priest, and the other priestly garments. God also gave Moses instructions on creating the incense, the anointing oil and the offerings for the sanctuary. All of these were blueprints that first existed in heaven but were eventually released to Moses when God's timing was right for it to be established in the earth. The specifics of all these things can be found in Exodus 25-31. The book of Hebrews also shares with us that the true tabernacle and mercy seat reside in heaven where God sits on His throne between the Cherubim, which is what the Ark of the Covenant displays. (see Hebrews 9:11-12).

KING DAVID:

King David was also apostolic because he established Mount Zion, which is a hill just outside the walls of the Old City of Jerusalem. It is actually older than the Old City of Jerusalem: It is the original city of David. Mount Zion existed in Heaven first (Hebrews 12:22-24), and David was God's instrument to establish it on earth (2 Samuel 5:7 and 1 Kings 8:1).

KING DAVID AND SOLOMON:

David received the heavenly blueprints for the temple. It was in David's heart to build this magnificent structure for God, and to house the Ark of the Covenant. But David wasn't allowed to build it, so he gave the heavenly blueprints to his son Solomon; and Solomon carried out the building and completion of the temple (see 1 Chronicles 28).

BE APOSTOLIC IN YOUR SPHERE OF INFLUENCE AND THE MARKETPLACE

Your eyes saw my substance, being yet unformed. And in Your book they all were written, The days fashioned for me, When as yet there were none of them. (Psalm 139:16)

We see the great things God did through others in the bible as they yielded themselves to Him. The wonderful things that God did with them, for them, and through them were already written in their destiny book before they came to the earth. So what about you? What is on your destiny scroll? What is written in your book of destiny?

How does God want to bring heaven into your sphere of influence? Your sphere of influence are the people and/or organizations within your personal circle, network and domain, that values your influence and opinion to the point that it can lead to effective change. How does God want to bring heaven (His desires, plans and original intent) into your sphere of influence? What are the strategies and blueprints that God wants to release through you and into your sphere of influence? As you seek God, He will give you directives, orders and instructions on what to do. God is using those who may not have a title in the church building, but have a major function and influence in the Kingdom and spirit realm. Many believers and intercessors have received heavenly decrees to declare as they do prayer walks.

You may ask what is a prayer walk? It is praying and interceding with love as you walk in and through the parks of your community, around malls, around your public schools, or in the parking lots of public schools, the boards of education building, courthouses, and legislative buildings in your community as you decree God's goodness and intent; releasing heaven into your sphere of influence. As we are faithful and consistent in our directives and assignments, our sphere of influence will begin to increase and spread as God gives us more greater responsibilities. He will show you how to do it, and when to do it. Along with those specific heavenly directives, the Host (Angel Armies) will be released by God to assist you. Certain angels are connected to different assignments in the earth. As we, by faith, step out into those directives and orders from Heaven, God will begin releasing those angels to assist us, to minister with and for us, and to co-labor with us.

SIDENOTE REGARDING PRINCIPALITIES: According to Ephesians 6:12, there are evil principalities and spiritual hosts of wickedness sitting on thrones of iniquities, in high places, over various territories on the earth. These beings give directives to the unclean spirits that work under them in a demonic hierarchy. Remember, the kingdom of darkness always attempts to duplicate and counterfeit the Kingdom of Light. I believe as we ascend to our mountain (government), AND live out of our mountain, we receive God's desire, plan, and original intent regarding the specific territory He wants us to repossess for the Kingdom of Light. We also receive directives, mandates, and orders through revelation. I want to encourage everyone to not put God in our traditional box regarding how we allow Him to get that revelation to us. The Lord could come Himself, he could send an angel, he could speak through a child, or it could be someone in a cloud of witnesses (who are part of the church). As we have discussed before, the mountain we ascend to as eagles, the Isaiah Company, is Mount Zion (Hebrews 12:22-24). That realm is in the heaven of heavens, the third heaven where we are seated in Heavenly Places in Christ.

*That the God of our Lord Jesus Christ, the Father of glory, may give to you the spirit of wisdom and revelation in the knowledge of Him, the eyes of your understanding being enlightened; that you may know what is the hope of His calling, what are the riches of the glory of His inheritance in the saints, and what is the exceeding greatness of His power toward us who believe, according to the working of His mighty power which He worked in Christ when **He raised Him from the dead and seated Him at His right hand in the heavenly places, far above all principality and power and might and dominion, and every name that is named, not only in this age but also in that which is to come. And He put all things under His feet, and gave Him to be head over all things to the church, which is His body, the fullness of Him who fills all in all.** (Ephesians 1:17-23)*

*Even when we were dead in trespasses, made us alive together with Christ (by grace you have been saved), and raised **us** up together, and made **us** sit together in the heavenly places in Christ Jesus. (Ephesians 2:5-6)*

This is the realm where all authority is placed under our feet. Just as an earthly ambassador has dual citizenship, while we physically live on the earth our citizenship is also in Heaven, Mount Zion, our place of authority. When we receive God's directives, we bypass and go above the high places where the evil principalities sit. We take the seat of authority in our heavenly place with, and in Christ, from where we receive our directives, blueprints and strategies to implement them in the earthly realm.

As we receive those heavenly strategies, we are not operating alone, just from the earth. Instead, we are operating from the authority of a higher realm, one which those principalities must respect and obey. I believe as we go in the Love of God to act and operate in those heavenly directives in obedience in our sphere of influence on earth first, this will play a key role in dethroning the demonic entities in their high places. This will affect regions in the earth, including our families, churches, neighborhoods, communities and governments. In scripture, we never saw Jesus, in His earthly ministry, go directly after principalities. He received His mandates and directives from the Father, and as He traveled to different regions executing those heavenly directives on earth, this ultimately led Him to the cross. Let's look at three examples from the bible: Two involving Jesus and one involving the Apostle Paul.

1) In Mark 5:1-20, coming to the other side of the sea after facing opposition from what I believe were evil spirits that ruled in that area through the air (the wind) and in the waters (the spirit of leviathan and dagon also works from the waters), which is the reason Jesus had to both rebuke the winds and speak peace to the water in Mark 4:39-50.

> **SIDENOTE:** Scripture references for leviathan can be found at Job 41, Psalm 74:13-14, Psalm 104:26 and Isaiah 27:1. Scripture reference for dagon is in 1 Samuel 5:1-8. Dagon is the god that the Philistines worshipped which has the appearance of a merman (half man and half fish).

When Jesus and his disciples crossed over the sea and "stepped" onto the land, "immediately" he met a man who dwelt night and day in the mountains and in the tombs. We found out earlier in chapter 2 of this book that mountains represent governments. So this man, who was possessed with legions of demons, dwelt in the governments (mountains) of that region. This possessed man had control and fear over the region because verse 4 said the people in that region often attempted to bind him with shackles and chains, but he always broke out of them; and no one could control him because the demons within him had control over the entire region through him. We don't see Jesus crossing over the sea, stepping onto the land and directly confronting and engaging the principality that had authority over that area in the heavenlies. Instead, Jesus took authority as He followed the directives of the Father. While crossing the sea, He executed authority over the spirits in the air and water as He crossed over the sea. And when He stepped out onto land on the other side, He executed authority in the earthly realm, casting Legion (the name of the demons) out of the man, and sending them into two thousand swine who were feeding near "the mountains," This led to the removal of the swine in that area for they immediately ran into the water and were drowned. The swine were not supposed to be in that area because according to Jewish Law they were considered unclean. Notice that the swine were feeding "near" the mountains. They were in close proximity to the government of that region while the man possessed with Legion dwelt in the mountains, the government of that area. Jesus, following His heavenly orders, being led of the Father, cast the legion of demons out of the man, and removed the two thousand swine. Now, Legion and the demons who ruled that area do not have a body to dwell in and work through (the man nor the swine). The scripture shows us that the principality over that region was devastated because of the fruit that followed from the loss of their income. Those who fed the swine told the people in the city and in the region. The people went out to see what happened. They came to Jesus and saw the man who had the legion sitting, clothed and in his right mind. Then they became fearful. The rule of the principality had warped their way of thinking. They should have been happy for the man and for themselves over no longer being in bondage to the fear and control that was over that region. But because the evil principality had been there for so long, I believe through the generations of the people that lived in that region, they came to tolerate it to the point where it became a way of life. Since there was now a vacuum (an empty spiritual void) due to the evil spirit not having a body or bodies to work through, the Lord commissioned the man who was freed from the demonic possession, to go and spread the news of the great things the Lord did for him and how Jesus had compassion on him. The scripture said the man proclaimed it in Decapolis, an area encompassing ten cities. History tells us that the Decapolis area experienced great revival from the gospel after Christ rose from the dead.

2) Colossians 2:15 shares with us that through the cross and resurrection of Jesus, He publicly embarrassed the evil powers and principalities by disarming and stripping away all of their weapons, along with their authority in the spirit world. So, Jesus executed all of this devastating and demoralizing destruction against the enemy in the spirit realm by fulfilling the Father's directives on earth (on the cross) and in hades, while His body was in the tomb three days and nights following His death.

3) The last example is found in Acts 16 where the Apostle Paul received directives in a night vision to go to Macedonia. Paul was obedient and left; and being led by Holy Spirit in boldness, he declared the good news of Jesus, which led to the salvation of Lydia and her household. Verse 16 shows that as Paul and others were going to prayer, they encountered a slave girl who had the spirit of

divination. It said this girl followed Paul for many days, operating in this spirit. Then the day came when Paul was moved in his spirit and received the directives to take authority over the spirit and cast it out. Remember, we only do what God leads us to do when He tells us to do it. This girl who was possessed with a python spirit was in the marketplace; and I believe she was directly connected to the principality that was over the city of Philippi at that time. The reason I believe this is true is because you can see the fruit that occurred following her deliverance. The owners who made a lot of money in the marketplace from her were furious. The whole city was disturbed. Even the magistrates who ran the court system were upset from this slave girl's deliverance that was connected to the evil principality over that city. So, in order to bring revival to the city of Philippi, the Apostle Paul had to execute heavenly directives in the earthly realm, which in turn affected the high places in that city.

It's vital to remember that assigned to those heavenly directives and mandates from God are the angels of the Lord and the Host of heaven, the angelic armies. They all work with us on earth and in the heavenly places. Some demonic principalities have become comfortable in their position because they may have been operating in that place for generations. But the church is now being informed about their tactics and abilities. The Isaiah Company is ascending, and all we have to do under God's directive is show up with the heavenly eviction papers. The territory belongs to us. And as we operate in our true identity, these iniquitous thrones will be overthrown, and heaven will rule there and over those regions as the church continues to bring heaven to earth. The thing the enemy fears the most is God's children coming to the knowledge of who we really are in Christ, and what we can really do through Christ.

Now Jericho was securely shut up because of the children of Israel; none went out, and none came in. And the Lord said to Joshua: "See! I have given Jericho into your hand, its king, and the mighty men of valor. You shall march around the city, all you men of war; you shall go all around the city once. This you shall do six days. And seven priests shall bear seven trumpets of rams' horns before the ark. But the seventh day you shall march around the city seven times, and the priests shall blow the trumpets. It shall come to pass, when they make a long blast with the ram's horn, and when you hear the sound of the trumpet that all the people shall shout with a great shout; then the wall of the city will fall down flat. And the people shall go up every man straight before him." Joshua 6:1-5

In Joshua 6, God revealed His intent regarding the city of Jericho. He had already given Jericho its king and their mighty men into Joshua's hands. God then proceeds to give Joshua the specific directives and instructions on how to accomplish what is on God's heart and mind. This is shown in Joshua 6:3-5.

> SIDENOTE: And it came to pass, when Joshua was by Jericho, that he lifted his eyes and looked, and behold, a Man stood opposite him with His sword drawn in His hand. And Joshua went to Him and said to Him, "Are You for us or for our adversaries? So He said, "No, but as Commander of the army of the Lord I have now come. And Joshua fell on his face to the earth and worshiped, and said to Him, "What does my Lord say to His servant?" Then the Commander of the Lord's army said to Joshua, "Take your sandal off your foot, for the place where you stand is holy." And Joshua did so. Joshua 5:13-15

We see that prior to Joshua receiving his specific directives, he experienced a supernatural encounter as he **lifted his eyes, looked into, and beheld** the supernatural realm. Looking at the city of Jericho in the natural, I am sure it seemed an intimidating and daunting sight, especially after feeling the pressure of leading God's people. So, I am sure this supernatural encounter reassured Joshua that the Lord was with him, that he was on the right path, and that the angelic armies were backing him up.

I want to drive this point home, I feel that the Lord wants to encourage us to not put Him in a box regarding how we receive the heavenly directives, strategies and blueprints. God may speak them directly into your spirit through Holy Spirit. The Lord may visit you Himself to share them with you. The Lord may send one of His messengers, an angel of the Lord, or a heavenly being, to share them with you. God is a supernatural God, and we are His supernatural children. He is challenging us to not put Him in a box regarding how He desires to communicate and reveal things to us. Don't limit Him. God doesn't want fear to hold back the good things and supernatural encounters He has for us. We need discernment, and we will discuss that in the next chapter.

In Joshua 6:6-20, we see Joshua demonstrating his faith in God through obediently following the Lord's instructions. The facts showed them that Jericho was extremely secured; and no one could go out or in. The truth (God's original intent and desire) said that Jericho had already been delivered to Joshua in the spirit, but Joshua had to walk out God's plan in the natural; and in time heaven's agenda was released into the earth (Jericho).

So, back to you. Is there a new revival or church model the Lord may want to release through you that will help usher in a visitation, a habitation, and a reformation of God's glory in the earth? Is there a new video game God wants to release through you that would bless the younger and older generations by bringing heaven to earth in the gaming industry? What new phone app does heaven want to release that will bring a solution to a problem? What new fashion, clothing line, jewelry design, new interface, new technology or source of energy does God want to release to the earth through His children to bless the peoples of the earth? What new invention or new business model does heaven want to release through you?

> SIDENOTE: The apostolic and entrepreneurial spirit are very similar, to the point that you are releasing something to the earth that has not existed before. And God wants us to engage the spirit of wisdom, prudence and the fear of the Lord, to merge the apostolic and entrepreneurship together, for us to receive the wealth of the wicked.

A good man leaves an inheritance to his children's children, but the sinner's wealth is laid up for the righteous. (Proverbs 13:22 ESV)

What is the marketplace? Merriam-Webster defines the marketplace as "the world of trade or economic activity: The everyday world."

The bible shows us that five of Jesus' first twelve apostles were called from within the marketplace by the Lord.

Matthew 4 gives us the account of two sets of brothers, Peter and Andrew, and James and John, being called by Jesus to follow Him into the ministry. Being in the commercial fishing industry when Jesus called them to follow Him, they came from an entrepreneurial background.

Matthew 9:9 shows Matthew being called to follow Jesus into the ministry from within the marketplace as he was collecting taxes. It is noteworthy that Jesus, our pattern and blueprint, didn't go into the synagogues or religious institutions of the day to call his first twelve apostles. Instead, through the leading of the Father, Jesus called five of the twelve apostles, while these men were in their vocation, in the marketplace realm, and poured the Kingdom of God into them. Ephesians 2:20 declares that we, the church, are built upon the foundation of the apostles and prophets, and we see that at least five of the twelve apostles were called while in the marketplace. At least four of those five had an entrepreneurial mindset. I believe as it was in the beginning of the foundation of the Church, so will it be now, and as we the church matures, we will have a major Kingdom influence and impact in the marketplace.

DISCERNMENT IN THE MARKETPLACE

It is strategic that the eagle faced government (the seer/prophetic nature) is needed and intended to work with the ox faced government (the apostolic) in the marketplace; realizing the enemy will not just idly sit back and allow your Kingdom advancement in the marketplace to go unchallenged. Instead, they will do everything in their power to challenge, deceive, hinder or stop you. The enemy will assign a Laban spirit against you just as Laban was assigned to manipulate Jacob in Genesis 28-31. The Prophetic (the eagle face), in the marketplace, will give us discernment against the Laban spirit's manipulation and deception, who desires to hinder and abort our Kingdom purpose and agenda in the marketplace. As we advance in offensive progression, God will give us the strategies to confront and defeat the enemies counterattacks in all areas of our lives, including in the marketplace.

APOSTOLIC HEALINGS

I believe every assignment we are destined to accomplish is on our destiny scroll (book), according to Psalm 139:16. I believe when we, as ascending eagles who live from our heavenly place in Christ, encounter a person on earth who needs a healing or creative miracle such as a person with a missing eye, insomnia, a person with a deformed arm, or with a headache, that we, as the Isaiah Company, can receive the download from God on how heaven sees that person. Through our natural eyes we may see the person as having a missing eye but heaven sees them as possessing two functional eyes. With our natural eyes we may see that person sitting up for hours at night desiring and wishing they could go to sleep, heaven sees them free and sleeping peacefully throughout the whole night (Psalm 127:2). With our natural eyes we may see the person with one deformed arm, but heaven sees that person with two functional arms. And heaven will see the other person with no headache. So, it's important that we connect with heaven to see what it sees so we can produce heaven on earth. The body parts that are in heaven for those people will be brought down by the angels of the Lord, as we stand as a gate and a door to release heaven to earth. These are what I call Apostolic Healings; for it is the term that the Lord whispered to my spirit. Remember, the apostolic are the sent ones who are bringing and manifesting heaven's atmosphere (culture) on earth, and we all have been commissioned by the Lord to go and do this.

*Later He appeared to the eleven as they sat at the table; and He rebuked their unbelief and hardness of heart, because they did not believe those who had seen Him after He had risen. And He said to them, "**Go** into all the world and preach the gospel to every creature. He who believes and is baptized will be saved; but he who does not believe will be condemned. And these signs will follow those who believe: **In My name** they will cast out demons; they will speak with new tongues; they will take up serpents; and if they drink anything deadly, it will by no means hurt them; **they will lay hands on the sick, and they will recover.**" So then, after the Lord had spoken to them, He was received up into heaven, and sat down at the right hand of God.* Mark 16:14-19

THE GARDEN OF EDEN, EARTH'S FIRST APOSTOLIC CENTER

The Lord God planted a garden eastward in Eden, and there He put the man whom He had formed. And out of the ground the Lord God made every tree grow that is pleasant to the sight and good for food. The tree of life was also in the midst of the garden, and the tree of the knowledge of good and evil. Now a river went out of Eden to water the garden, and from there it parted and became four riverheads. The name of the first is Pishon; it is the one which skirts the whole land of Havilah, where there is gold. And the gold of that land is good. Bdellium and the onyx stone are there. The name of the second river is Gihon; it is the one which goes around the whole land of Cush. The name of the third river is Hiddekel; it is the one which goes toward the east of Assyria. The fourth river is the Euphrates. Then the Lord God took the man and put him in the Garden of Eden to tend and keep it. Genesis 2:8-15

The first apostolic center or apostolic hub was the Garden of Eden. Even before God created the Garden of Eden for Adam, God had His own garden, called Eden.

You were in Eden, the garden of God; Every precious stone was your covering: The sardius, topaz, and diamond, Beryl, onyx, and jasper, Sapphire, turquoise, and emerald with gold. The workmanship of your timbrels and pipes Was prepared for you on the day you were created. Ezekiel 28:13

Eden is God's own intimate garden.

> **SIDENOTE:** That's where the desire within man (humanity) to have their personal gardens originated from. Many people love gardening, and many kings of the past and current leaders of nations have their own private gardens.

According to Ezekiel 28:13, lucifer had access to Eden in heaven, and verse 13 lists the different stones that covered lucifer including onyx (a precious stone) and gold, which is in the Garden of Eden that was made for man. We also see different accounts of the onyx stone and gold in heaven throughout scripture.

The onyx stone is also the fifth foundation of the wall in the Heavenly Jerusalem.

The twelve foundations of the wall were adorned with every kind of precious stone—the first was jasper, the second sapphire, the third agate, the fourth emerald, **the fifth onyx***, the sixth carnelian, the seventh chrysolite, the eighth beryl, the ninth topaz, the tenth chrysoprase, the eleventh turquoise, and the twelfth amethyst.* (Revelation 21:19-20 TPT)

Also in Revelation 21, we see gold in heaven.

Around the throne were twenty-four thrones, and on the thrones I saw twenty-four elders sitting, clothed in white robes; and they had **crowns of gold** *on their heads.* Revelation 4:4

The construction of its wall was of jasper; and the city was **pure gold***, like clear glass.* Revelation 21:18

The twelve gates were twelve pearls: each individual gate was of one pearl. And the street of the city was **pure gold***, like transparent glass.* (Revelation 21:21)

In Revelation 22 we also see the River of Life flowing from God as He sits on the throne.

And he showed me a pure river of water of life, clear as crystal, proceeding from the throne of God and of the Lamb. In the middle of its street, and on either side of the river, was the tree of life, which bore twelve fruits, each tree yielding its fruit every month. The leaves of the tree were for the healing of the nations. And there shall be no more curse, but the throne of God and of the Lamb shall be in it, and His servants shall serve Him. Revelation 22:1-3

So we see some parallels between what is in Heaven (including Eden, the garden of God) and what was in the Garden of Eden, made for Adam, and its surrounding areas; the Garden of Eden's sphere of influence.

Now a river went out of Eden to water the garden, and from there it parted and became four riverheads. (Genesis 2:10)

The river of God is heaven's lifeline to earth. The river of life comes directly from God as He sits on His throne, as we see in Revelation 22:1. Then the river flows into Eden, God's garden, before flowing into the Garden of Eden which God made for man, Adam's garden. I believe that because the river of life flowed into the Garden of Eden, the life of God that was in the river also released God's nature and goodness, producing gold and onyx. Those are just two things mentioned, but I believe there were many more of heaven's manifestations there. No curse was there, establishing the culture and the atmosphere of the blessing. Then we see that from the Garden of Eden this river split into four branching rivers. Genesis 2:11-14 provides some information on the lands that the four branching rivers ran through. It shows us how the lands surrounding the Garden of Eden had good gold, onyx stones, and bdellium. I believe the surrounding lands had these precious resources because of their close proximity to the blessing in the Garden of Eden, and the four branching rivers carried the goodness of God's nature in it. Remember, this all occurred before the fall of man.

I believe God, in the book of Genesis, gives us a blueprint and a pattern of how an apostolic center or apostolic hub looks, and how it is intended to function. We cannot have an apostolic hub (center) without God's directive, mandate, authority, and power. Remember, the purpose of the apostolic is to release heaven (God's goodness) to earth.

Then God said, "Let Us make man in Our image, according to Our likeness; **let them have dominion over the fish of the sea, over the birds of the air, and over the cattle, over all the earth and over every creeping thing that creeps on the earth.**" *So God created man in His own image; in the image of God He created him;* **male and female He created them.** *Then* **God blessed them,** *and God said to them,* **"Be fruitful and multiply; fill the earth and subdue it; have dominion over the fish of the sea, over the birds of the air, and over every living thing that moves on the earth."** (Genesis 1:26-28)

Man was created in God's own image, both male and female, at the time of the release of the mandate. So, it's important for an apostolic hub (center) to have a specific mandate from God to be on that unique apostolic hub's book of destiny. Remember, all our heavenly scrolls are unique. The actual heavenly directives and strategies will look different, but the overall and ultimate goal is to bring heaven to earth within that apostolic center's sphere of influence. That is why it is so important to receive the destiny scroll from Heaven. Along with the mandate comes a release of the grace needed to accomplish this, which is: God's enabling power, all of Heaven's army, the angels assigned to that scroll and the mandate to co-labor with those fulfilling this apostolic mandate. Notice that included in the mandate was man being given dominion over all the animals, every creeping thing, and over every living thing that moves on the earth; and that included Lucifer. Also included in the mandate is the key and strategy over any interference from the enemy.

AN APOSTOLIC VESSEL

But the angel said to her, "Do not be afraid, Mary; you have found favor with God. **You will conceive and give birth to a son,** *and you are to call him Jesus. He will be great and will be called the Son of the Most High. The*

Lord God will give him the throne of his father David, and he will reign over Jacob's descendants forever; his kingdom will never end." "How will this be," Mary *asked the angel, "since I am a virgin"? The angel answered, "The Holy Spirit will come on you, and the power of the Most High will overshadow you. So the holy one* **to be born** *will be called the Son of God.* (Luke 1:30-35)

Mothers are apostolic by nature. God designed and enabled the body of a mother to bring forth a child. A mother gives birth to something that was first in the spirit realm into the natural realm; a being that never existed on the earth before. A mother is an apostolic vessel for God, who releases to the earth a speaking spirit embodied in a male or female earth suit (baby's body). This spirit being who comes into earth, inside the womb of the mother at conception has the following two things:

A BOOK (SCROLL) OF DESTINY:

For You formed my inward parts; You covered me in my mother's womb. I will praise You, for I am fearfully and wonderfully made; Marvelous are Your works, And that my soul knows very well. My frame was not hidden from You, When I was made in secret, And skillfully wrought in the lowest parts of the earth. Your eyes saw my substance, being yet unformed. And in Your book they all were written, The days fashioned for me, When as yet there were none of them. How precious also are Your thoughts to me, O God! How great is the sum of them! (Psalm 139:13-17)

AT LEAST ONE ANGEL OF THE LORD ASSIGNED:

"Take heed that you do not despise one of these little ones, for I say to you that in heaven their angels always see the face of My Father who is in heaven. (Matthew 18:10)

HANNAH WAS INTENTIONAL

And she was in bitterness of soul, and prayed to the Lord and wept in anguish. Then she made a vow and said, "O Lord of hosts, if You will indeed look on the affliction of Your maidservant and remember me, and not forget Your maidservant, but will give Your maidservant a male child, then I will give him to the Lord all the days of his life, and no razor shall come upon his head." (1 Samuel 1:10-11)

Hannah was barren and unable to bear children. Despite this physical challenge, Hannah realized that she was apostolic in the role she could play in bringing God's plan to the earth by birthing a child who would be offered back to the Lord. Due to her vow to the Lord, she birthed Samuel, who became a powerful seer prophet. He would go on to anoint the first human king of Israel, Saul, and then King David, the man after God's own heart.

Behold, children are a heritage from the Lord, The fruit of the womb is a reward. (Psalm 127:3)

God has wonderfully and uniquely equipped a mother to physically bring forth a spirit being from heaven, wrapped in an earth suit (our bodies). And this in fact is Apostolic!

The Love of God is the Thriving Force Within the Government of the Ox (1 Corinthians 13)

ACTIVATION:

Each of them had four faces and four wings. Their legs were straight and their feet were like a calf's hoof, and they gleamed like burnished bronze. Under their wings on their four sides were human hands. As for the faces and wings of the four of them, their wings touched one another; their faces did not turn when they moved, each went straight forward. As for the form of their faces, each had the face of a man; all four had the face of a lion on the right and the face of a bull (ox) on the left, and all four had the face of an eagle. Such were their faces. Their wings were spread out above; each had two touching another being, and two covering their bodies. And each went straight forward; wherever the spirit was about to go, they would go, without turning as they went. (Ezekiel 1:6-12 NASB)

I want you to use the above scripture as a door and gateway as you engage in meditation and focus. Remember, the Word is alive, so see yourself there. In this activation, I want you to specifically focus on the face of the ox. Look at the features, the colors, and the motions. Listen to the sounds, remembering that sounds have a frequency in the spirit. Ask Holy Spirit to reveal the ox's government and anointing He desires you to walk in on the earth. Journal what you see, hear, observe and feel.

DISCUSSION POINTS:

1) What aspects of the face of man's government are brought out in this chapter, and how do you think it relates to you?

2) What aspects of the face of the eagle's government are brought out in this chapter, and how do you think it relates to you?

3) What aspects of the face of the lion's government are brought out in this chapter, and how do you think it relates to you?

4) What aspects of the face of the ox's government are brought out in this chapter and how do you think it relates to you?

5) How are the four face governments effective in the area of dealing with principalities?

ENDNOTE:

https://www.scienceabc.com/nature/secret-behind-lions-roar.html

CHAPTER 4

CONVERGENCE AND SYNERGY OF THE FOUR FACE GOVERNMENT: MATURITY, ENCOUNTERS AND DISCERNMENT

Then I looked, and behold, a whirlwind was coming out of the north, a great cloud with raging fire engulfing itself; and brightness was all around it and radiating out of its midst like the color of amber, out of the midst of the fire. Also from within it came the likeness of four living creatures. And this was their appearance: they had the likeness of a man. Each one had four faces, and each one had four wings. Their legs were straight, and the soles of their feet were like the soles of calves' feet. They sparkled like the color of burnished bronze. The hands of a man were under their wings on their four sides; and each of the four had faces and wings. Their wings touched one another. The creatures did not turn when they went, but each one went straight forward. As for the likeness of their faces, each had the face of a man; each of the four had the face of a lion on the right side, each of the four had the face of an ox on the left side, and each of the four had the face of an eagle. Thus were their faces. Their wings stretched upward; two wings of each one touched one another, and two covered their bodies. And each one went straight forward; they went wherever the spirit wanted to go, and they did not turn when they went. (Ezekiel 1:4-12)

As for their rims, they were so high they were awesome; and their rims were full of eyes, all around the four of them. When the living creatures went, the wheels went beside them; and when the living creatures were lifted up from the earth, the wheels were lifted up. (Ezekiel 1:18-19)

Before the throne there was a sea of glass, like crystal. And in the midst of the throne, and around the throne, were four living creatures full of eyes in front and in back. The first living creature was like a lion, the second living creature like a calf, the third living creature had a face like a man, and the fourth living creature was like a flying eagle. The four living creatures, each having six wings, were full of eyes around and within. And they do not rest day or night, saying: "Holy, holy, holy, Lord God Almighty, Who was and is and is to come!" (Revelation 4:6-8)

THE CHERUBIM REFLECT THOSE MATURE CHILDREN WHO BEAR GOD'S IMAGE IN CHRIST

Before we go further let's briefly go over what a Cherub is. It's worth noting that Cherub is singular while Cherubim are plural. This will be an important distinction as we journey together in this chapter. Some describe the Cherubim as heavenly beings that are part of the angelic hierarchy. While they are certainly beings in the spiritual realm, the Bible does not teach this one way or the other. One thing we do know is that in scripture these heavenly beings are connected to the glory of God. Contrary to traditional teaching stating that Lucifer was an archangel, there is no biblical proof of that. Instead, Lucifer aka Satan is referred to as "the anointed cherub that covereth" before his fall. Cherubim were placed at the east of the garden of Eden after the fall of Adam to guard the way to the tree of life which had God's glory on it. We will discuss this in more depth later in this chapter.

Ezekiel 28:11-17 details that God created Lucifer as a beautiful cherub. This passage describes how Lucifer looked when he was first created. Scripture states he was perfect in beauty, covered with nine precious stones along with gold. He also contained a variety of musical instruments in his body, a sort of living orchestra.

The book of Ezekiel also gives other accounts of God's Cherubim during his heavenly encounters in Ezekiel 1:1-14, 22-24, and 10:3-22. The cherubim are described with having one head with four faces, which consisted of an ox, eagle, lion and the face of a man. These cherubim also had four wings and unlike lucifer who was covered with nine precious stones when he was created, these cherubim are covered with eyes all over their being. These encounters in Ezekiel's encounters were awesome, powerful, and many would even consider frightening with the fear of the Lord.

We also see these four living creatures in Revelation 4:6-10 and once again they are around the throne with these same four faces- lion, ox, eagle, and man.

Also we see in scriptures that the Lord sits in heaven between the Cherubim.

Give ear, O Shepherd of Israel, you who lead Joseph like a flock. You who are enthroned upon the cherubim, shine forth. (Psalm 80:1 ESV)

The Lord reigns; let the peoples tremble! He sits enthroned upon the cherubim; let the earth quake! (Psalm 99:1 ESV)

The Cherubim have several functions in the bible such as carrying the transportable throne of God (Psalm 18:10), covering and guarding the glory in Eden (Ezekiel 28:14), guarding the Garden of Eden where they are accompanied with a living flaming sword (Genesis 3:24), being in close proximity to God (Revelation 4), and following the glory of God (Ezekiel 1:12). The Cherubim are closely associated and connected to the glory of the Lord. I believe they cover and guard the the glory of God as He sits on his throne.

As we have shared, the cherubim are connected to God's glory as the several spiritual encounters in Ezekiel records. We also see this with Lucifer who, as a cherub was connected to the glory in Eden, the Garden of God, prior to Adam being created.

THE CHERUBIM AND THE ARK OF COVENANT

We also have the ark of the Covenant which housed the bread, tablets of the law, and Aaron's rod that budded. This is a type pointing to Christ, and us; redeemed man. The ark was God's earthly prototype that housed His raw presence, His glory.

*"You shall make a mercy seat of pure gold; two and a half cubits shall be its length and a cubit and a half its width. [18] And you shall make two cherubim of gold; of hammered work you shall make them at the two ends of the mercy seat. [19] Make one cherub at one end, and the other cherub at the other end; you shall make the cherubim at the two ends of it of one piece with the mercy seat. [20] And the cherubim shall stretch out their wings above, covering the mercy seat with their wings, and they shall face one another; the faces of the cherubim shall be toward the mercy seat. [21] You shall put the mercy seat on top of the ark, and in the ark you shall put the Testimony that I will give you. [22] **And there I will meet with you, and I will speak with you from above the mercy seat, from between the two cherubim** which are on the ark of the Testimony, about everything which I will give you in commandment to the children of Israel.* (Exodus 25:17-22 NKJV)

The top of the ark had a cherub on both sides between the mercy seat, again showing us they are connected to the glory. The Lord told Moses that it would be "there" between the two cherubim on the Ark of the Covenant that God would speak with him. I believe Jesus was the living fulfillment of the Ark of the Covenant when He walked the earth. Each piece of furniture and design given by God to Moses within the Tabernacle, including the Ark of the Covenant and the Veil, was pointing to Jesus Christ. And because we are in Christ, we have **access to the revelation** of what Jesus fulfilled, along with **the opportunity, privilege and responsibility to walk and live it out** through the glory that is also within us and upon us.

But we all, with unveiled face, beholding as in a mirror the glory of the Lord, are being transformed into the same image from glory to glory, just as by the Spirit of the Lord. (2 Corinthians 3:18 NKJV)

Today, as we are in Christ, we the body of Christ which consists of you and myself are heaven's demonstration of the Ark of the Covenant on the earth today. Instead of two stone tablets we have the law of God in our hearts (our spirits), instead of the pot of manna that fell from the sky we have the Living bread inside of us through our Lord Jesus, and instead of Aaron's rod that budded through Holy Spirit we have inside of us the glorious resurrection power that raised Jesus from the dead.

The Ark of the Covenant had gold overlaying the shittim wood. We, the Children of God and joint heirs of Jesus, have the power of God's anointing and glory resting upon us (our human bodies) (Acts 1:8). The gold represents the Power of God and the shittim wood of the Ark represents our humanity.

So we see here that God talked to Moses between the two cherubim on the Ark of the Covenant.

THE CHERUBIM AND THE VEIL (CURTAIN)

*"You shall make a veil woven of blue, purple, and scarlet thread, and fine woven linen. It shall be woven with an **artistic design of cherubim**."* (Exodus 26:31 NKJV)

We see in the Old Testament the actual veil (curtain) that separated and protected sinful man had the artistic design of the cherubim on it. Once a year the high priest had to go through the veil and enter into God's glory. That level of glory that the high priest experienced once a year would not and could not be experienced by anyone else on the earth due to God's power, energy, holiness and the requirements it took to experience that heavenly glory for even such a short span of time. In going through the curtain supernaturally, the high priest also had to go through the artistic design of the cherubim on the veil before accessing the Ark of the Covenant on the other side of the veil. So, to enter God's presence man in the Old Testament had to go through the cherubim (the image on veil), which I believe was designed to help man get back in the right heavenly identity and government.

> SIDENOTE: The high priest had to go through the veil which had the artist design of Cherubim (more than one), and once he went through, he engaged the Ark of the Covenant which was infused with the glory of God. The Ark also included Cherubim as part of its heavenly design.

THE CHERUBIM, FLAMING SWORD, AND THE WAY TO THE TREE OF LIFE

*So He drove out the man; and He placed **cherubim** at the east of the garden of Eden, **and a flaming sword** which turned every way, **to guard the way** to the tree of life.* (Genesis 3:24 NKJV)

The Lord here placed more than one cherub at the east of the Garden of Eden, along with a flaming sword. In the past I believed God placed an angel there who had a flaming sword in his hand. But the word said it was Cherubim who were placed there and the flaming sword was there to guard the way to the tree of life. It is worth noting that the flaming sword turned every way.

The New Living Translation says Genesis 3:24 like this, *"After sending them out, the Lord God stationed mighty cherubim to the east of the Garden of Eden. And he placed a flaming sword that flashed back and forth to guard the way to the tree of life."*

The New American Standard Bible states Genesis 3:24 like this, *"So He drove the man out; and at the east of the garden of Eden He stationed the cherubim and the flaming sword which turned every direction to guard the way to the tree of life."*

I believe it's safe to say there was no getting past the flaming sword if you desired to get back on the way to the tree of life. I believe the flaming sword was a heavenly living creature with purpose and a function, which was to guard the way to the tree of life along with the mighty cherubim. So in order for man to access "the way" to the tree of life, they would have to go through both the cherubim and through the fire of the flaming sword. Remember the Prophet Isaiah also had an encounter with fire in Isaiah 6. God placed the cherubim and flaming sword there for our good and for our eternal protection; to prevent a sinful man from partaking of the tree of life while in his sinful state with a spirit that was dead to God, which would have led to man existing in that state of unfulfillment for eternity as a sort of walking corpse. This state was never God's original intent for His most prized and loved creation, man. The flaming sword was there to help transform and change us; as it is in the natural, so it is in the spirit, even more so.

> SIDENOTE: Genesis 5:21 says "And Enoch walked with God; and he was not, for God took him." By way of intimate fellowship with God, could encountering the way of the flaming sword and Cherubim been the way that Enoch took in order to be taken away without physically dying?

In the natural fire transforms the natural elements it encounters. It doesn't eliminate the matter, it transforms it into a different form of existence. After matter encounters fire that object is never the same as it was before its encounter. In many cases precious metals such as gold are refined and purified by fire which causes the impurities to rise to the top where they can be skimmed off. Therefore, fire plays a vital role in authenticating the value of pure gold. God compares us to gold, and likewise there are seasons where we have to go through a refining process before we can be put on display for his glory. Of course, this excludes objects that are intentionally designed to be fireproof or withstand high temperatures.

Jesus is the baptizer of Fire and the Lord of Hosts (Angel Armies)

*I baptize you with water for repentance, but he who is coming after me is mightier than I, whose sandals I am not worthy to carry. He will baptize you with the Holy Spirit **and** fire.* (Matthew 3:11 ESV)

*And when the day of Pentecost had fully come, they were all assembled together in one place,² When suddenly there came a sound from heaven like the rushing of a violent tempest blast, and it filled the whole house in which they were sitting.³ And there appeared to them tongues **resembling fire**, which were separated and distributed and which **settled on each one of them.** ⁴ And **they were all filled (diffused throughout their souls) with the Holy Spirit** and began to speak in other (different, foreign) languages (tongues), as the Spirit kept giving them clear and loud expression [in each tongue in appropriate words].* (Acts 2:1-4 AMPC)

While I believe we the church have experienced a certain aspect of fire through the baptism of Holy Spirit, I believe there is a baptism of fire that we have not yet fully received that is reserved for us, and this baptism of fire will transform us to something that is even more like Christ. In Acts 2 it shows us that the baptism of Holy Spirit filled them then diffused or spread from the spirit man to the souls and affected the natural man; and the fire that came rested or settled on them. I believe this baptism of fire will do what Holy Spirit did in Acts 2, filling us to the brim and dispersing, then spreading to our soulish man to burn anything in us contrary to God's holiness. I believe this will be done with God's love, joy and the spirit of the fear of the Lord. I also believe when we experience this baptism with fire that we will be unrecognizable compared to our current version of ourselves.

In the year that King Uzziah died, [in a vision] I saw the Lord sitting upon a throne, high and lifted up, and the skirts of His train filled the [most holy part of the] temple. ²Above Him stood the seraphim; each had six wings: with two [each] covered his [own] face, and with two [each] covered his feet, and with two [each] flew. ³ And one cried to another and said, Holy, holy, holy is the Lord of hosts; the whole earth is full of His glory! ⁴ And the foundations of the thresholds shook at the voice of him who cried, and the house was filled with smoke. ⁵ Then said I, Woe is me! For I am undone and ruined, because I am a man of unclean lips, and I dwell in the midst of a people of unclean lips; for my eyes have seen the King, the Lord of hosts! ⁶ Then flew one of the seraphim [heavenly beings] to me, having a live coal in his hand which he had taken with tongs from off the altar; ⁷ And with it he touched my mouth and said, Behold, this has touched your lips; your iniquity and guilt are taken away, and your sin is completely atoned for and forgiven. (Isaiah 6:1-7 AMPC)

> **SIDENOTE:** I believe this baptism of fire will include the work of Holy Spirit along with the ministry of the Seraphim angelic beings who are called the fiery or burning ones, which are also around God's throne which contains his glory of fire.

You make your messengers into winds of the Spirit and all of your ministers become flames of fire. (Psalm 104:4 TPT)

And about his angels he says, "I make my angels swift winds, and my ministers fiery flames." (Hebrews 1:7 TPT)

And He said to him, "Most assuredly, I say to you, hereafter you shall see heaven open, and the angels of God ascending and descending upon the Son of Man." (John 1:51 NKJV)

having become as much superior to angels as the name he has inherited is more excellent than theirs For to which of the angels did God ever say, "You are my Son, today I have begotten you"? Or again, "I will be to him a father, and he shall be to me a son"? And again, when he brings the firstborn into the world, he says, "Let all God's angels worship him." (Hebrews 1:4-6 ESV)

When we are in an intimate relationship with Christ He becomes THE way to the Father, to the glory, and to the tree of Life; and through him, our baptizer of fire, we are transformed and through Him, our Lord of Hosts, we have free access through the Cherubim that guard the way to the Tree of Life, unlike in Genesis when Adam was removed from the

Garden. The Cherubim tribe of angelic beings is under the Lordship of Jesus Christ.

Excluding Enoch, according to the scriptures, everyone died from Adam to the time of Moses, even though they didn't disobey God on the same level that Adam did.

Still, everyone died—from the time of Adam to the time of Moses—even those who did not disobey an explicit commandment of God, as Adam did. ***Now Adam is a symbol, a representation of Christ, who was yet to come.*** (Romans 5:14 NLT emphasis added)

Jesus said to him, "I am the way, the truth, and the life. No one comes to the Father except through Me. (John 14:6 NKJV)

God already had the man Christ Jesus in mind before He formed Adam out of the dust of the ground. The Word was already there; God used the Word to create all things, and the Word became flesh (John 1:1-3, 14). The first Adam that God formed in the Garden of Eden out of the dust of the ground was a symbol and representation of the Christ, the last Adam; who in God's mind was already born, had died, was buried, went to hell, rose from the dead on the third day, ascended back to heaven, and then sat down before the foundations of the world (in Eternity Past).

Because of this Jesus Christ is not just a way to the Father but He is THE only way to the Father. Also Jesus is the new and living way back to the glory, and the tree of Life. Therefore, brethren, since we have full freedom and confidence to enter into the [Holy of] Holies [by the power and virtue] in the blood of Jesus, [20] *By this fresh (new) and living way which He initiated and dedicated and opened for us through the separating curtain (veil of the Holy of Holies), that is, through His flesh,* [21] *And since we have [such] a great and wonderful and noble Priest [Who rules] over the house of God,* [22] *Let us all come forward and draw near with true (honest and sincere) hearts in unqualified assurance and absolute conviction engendered by faith (by that leaning of the entire human personality on God in absolute trust and confidence in His power, wisdom, and goodness), having our hearts sprinkled and purified from a guilty (evil) conscience and our bodies cleansed with pure water.* (Hebrews 10:19-22 AMPC)

"He who has an ear, let him hear what the Spirit says to the churches. To him who overcomes I will give to eat from the tree of life, which is in the midst of the Paradise of God." (Revelation 2:7 NKJV)

Blessed are those who do His commandments, that they may have the right to the tree of life, and may enter through the gates into the city. (Revelation 22:14 NKJV)

Remember the cherubim's connection to the glory? They are protectors of the glory, and we see in John 1:14 that Jesus was, and is the fullness of the Father's glory in flesh.

And the Word (Christ) became flesh (human, incarnate) and tabernacled (fixed His tent of flesh, lived awhile) among us; and we [actually] saw His glory (His honor, His majesty), such glory as an only begotten son receives from his father, full of grace (favor, loving-kindness) and truth. (John 1:14 AMPC)

Throughout scripture we see the Cherubs are very closely associated with the glory, whether in heaven (around God's throne) or on earth (in Ezekiel's encounters), and I believe this also applies in Christ's life and for us, because the glory of God has the capacity to dwell in us and upon us, as it does in Christ because we are the body of Christ in the earth.

*Love has been perfected among us in this: that we may have boldness in the day of judgment; because **as He is, so are we in this world**.* (1 John 4:17 NKJV)

He bowed the heavens also, and came down With darkness under His feet And He rode upon a cherub, and flew; He flew upon the wings of the wind. He made darkness His secret place; His canopy around Him was dark waters And thick clouds of the skies From the brightness before Him, His thick clouds passed with hailstones and coals of fire. (Psalm 18:9-12)

We even see Cherubim carrying the glorious transportable throne of God and how the glory of God flies upon the wings of the wind (Angelic presence).

Of the angels he says, "He makes his angels winds, and his ministers a flame of fire." (Hebrews 1:7 ESV)

Even though Adam was formed first in the earth, as I previously stated, he was a symbol and representation of something greater that would come; the man Jesus Christ.

I believe this same principle also applies to us, the manifested children of God, in our relationship to the Cherubim. Just as Adam was created first with Christ in mind as the ultimate blueprint, I also believe when the cheribum were first created in their awesome function in the heavens that God had us, His children, in mind for us to express the government of four faces as part of our identity in Christ.

The beginning of this chapter started with the scriptures detailing the two Cherubim encounters in Ezekiel 1 and Revelation 4. We have shared how the four faces (Lion, Ox, Eagle, and Man) connected to these Cherubim reflect and point to the government that the Children of God are destined to walk in. Also, some other similarities between the Cherubim in the scriptures and the children of God are these:

1) Both accounts make reference to these heavenly creatures **having eyes all over them**. We determined that the eagle face represents the prophetic and our seer nature; and we touched on what our seer nature consists of, and that the prophet Isaiah was called the eagle-eye prophet. I also believe the eyes throughout the bodies of these heavenly creatures confirms our seer nature, and us seeing in the spirit realm thereby seeing as God sees, from His perspective as children of God and the Isaiah Company in the earthly realm.

2) These accounts also reference that their **feet were like oxen hooves**. So we determined that the ox represented the apostolic government. The two main things an ox needs to perform its function in the field are strength and his feet (hooves). Our feet should have shoes that make us prepared to share the gospel of peace according to Ephesians 6:16. I believe also that our feet are designed to be apostolic, so no matter where they tread upon, we release heaven on earth as we tread the ground and tread our enemies.

> SIDENOTE: It doesn't matter the type of terrain we are treading on, we just have to make sure it's the land that the Lord specifically told us we can have. In Genesis 15:18-21 God gave Abraham the dimensions of the land, and as long as Abraham stayed within the boundaries of the land that God promised him, God covenanted to give him and his seed that land, no matter who was occupying the land. If Abraham had proceeded to pass those specific land dimensions or boundaries, then God would not be covenanted to back up Abraham in the land outside of the covenant. Men like Moses, Joshua and David could confidently fight giants who were physically much larger than them because those giants were in the covenanted land given to Abraham and his descendants. But if Moses, Joshua and David ventured into the territory outside of the covenant and fought the giants there, that could have led to their destruction. This is also life and death for us. We are only to confront and drive out the enemy from the territory God has assigned to us, if we venture outside of our assigned territory, it could lead to negative consequences for us and our families. This is why Jesus only did what He saw His father do and say what he heard His Father say. There is power and protection under true submission to God.

3) Also, the two scriptural accounts revealed that the Cherubim **stood upright as a man** and had **the hands of a man** under its wings on their four sides. I believe our posture in the earth is important if we are to operate in God's authority. Also, it is noted in this account that the Cherubim's posture in heaven were identified with standing as a man (a redeemed man from Heaven). Let me ask you again, do you see yourself as Heaven sees you? Also, the hands of Heaven (God) in the earthly realm are us, the children of God (humanity). We have been delegated to be God's mouthpiece, His feet and His hands in the earth. We are the Body of Christ.

ACTIVATION:

In this engagement I want you to read and mediate on Ezekiel 1 and Revelation 4, focusing on the heavenly creatures having eyes all over them, having their feet like oxen hooves, standing upright as a man, with the hands of a man. In this engagement, as you meditate ask the Lord how these different features relate to you in operating in God's power. Journal what you observe, hear, and feel.

The Cherubim are nothing to play with. They are awesome, powerful and fascinating beings. Their role in the government of God and their closeness to the Glory of God is to be honored, but not worshipped. Honor is what all beings in the Kingdom of God (in Heaven and Earth) live by. So we honor the Cherub and every heavenly creature that God has created, and the purpose He created them for. But as it is said in Psalm 8:5 NLT:

"Yet you made them (man) only a little lower than God and crowned them with glory and honor."

God has made born again man in God's class (classification and family), and I believe the children of God are the only creation who have that identity and authority in creation. Similar to the Cherubim, we are glory chasers, glory keepers and glory protectors. But unlike the Cherubim, we are children of God, and God's nature and glory resides in us not only upon us, like it does a Cherub.

*Grace and peace be multiplied to you in the knowledge of God and of Jesus our Lord, as His divine power has given to us all things that pertain to life and godliness, through the knowledge of Him who called us by glory and virtue, by which have been given to us exceedingly great and precious promises, that through these **you may be partakers of the divine nature**, having escaped the corruption that is in the world through lust.*

The divine nature in 2 Peter 1 enables supernatural birthing, growth (by germination or expansion), and gives us distinctive supernatural native uniqueness, characteristics, and strength like Father God our Daddy. So we have God's DNA in us that consists of His glory dwelling inside of us.

But we all, with unveiled face, beholding as in a mirror the glory of the Lord, are being transformed into the same image from glory to glory, just as by the Spirit of the Lord. (2 Corinthians 3:18)

So if a Cherub is connected to the glory of God, then a cherub is also connected to the glory of God that is within and upon us; yes that same glory that transforms us as we continually behold it. This is one way our nature and identity as children of God differs from a Cherub. Our identity and nature is found in our heavenly Daddy's glory and Father God's glory unlocks who we really are. The cherubim guards and covers the glory, goes before the glory, and follows the glory. They see different aspects of God in the glory, which keeps them in awe of God, but they are not transformed into the glory to the degree that we, the children of God are because they do not carry God's DNA as we do

His divine power has granted to us all things that pertain to life and godliness, through the knowledge of him who called us to his own glory and excellence, by which he has granted to us his precious and very great promises, so that through them you may **become partakers of the divine nature**, *having escaped from the corruption that is in the world because of sinful desire.* (2 Peter 1:3-4 ESV)

CHERUB ENCOUNTERS

We see in the books of Ezekiel and Revelation that these types of encounters are biblical. First, I want to emphasize that we are not to seek spiritual encounters because a zeal for only spiritual encounters can open you up to deception.

> SIDENOTE: We are to seek the Lord and pursue Him. Out of our intimate and passionate pursuit of the Lord will flow heavenly encounters with Him, angels, and heavenly beings; and this also includes encountering the Cherubim in the heavenly places in Christ.

Some believers are already forerunners in what I am going to share. There are believers who have experienced Cherub encounters as the created glorious atmospheres birthed from consistent intense prayer, praise, prophetic and ascension worship. In this type of atmosphere, the glory of God is manifested, creating a habitation where God's manifested and intimate presence (His glory) can readily be revealed. Psalm 18:10 states that God rides on the Cherubim and flies; so when God's glory (His manifested presence) comes the Cherubim accompany Him. So we shouldn't be alarmed or surprised that out of an intimate relationship with God we encounter heavenly realms and angelic beings such as the Seraph and the Cherub. I believe that as many more sons and daughters go deeper into intimacy with the Lord and ascend, we will experience more of these types of encounters with the Cherub due to the season we are in. I believe one of the reasons we will have these types of encounters will be a sign that this four face government has been fully released to the Church, who carries the glory of God inside of us.

DISCERNING THE SUPERNATURAL

For such are false apostles, deceitful workers, transforming themselves into apostles of Christ. And no wonder! For satan himself transforms himself into an angel of light. Therefore it is no great thing if his ministers also transform themselves into ministers of righteousness, whose end will be according to their works. (2 Corinthians 11:13-15)

Below are a few steps we can keep in mind whenever we receive a prophetic word, a revelation, or a supernatural encounter.

1) Does it agree and align with the plumb line, the revealed Word of God in the Bible? If not, then you have no need to go any further in discernment. Please keep in mind that your mindset is not the revealed word of God. A true revelation of the Word of God, prophecy or supernatural encounter may indeed contradict,

challenge and offend your mindset (how you think), or your paradigm of the Word of God. Mindsets are a product of our soulish man, and we are admonished to continually be renewed (stretched) in our mind through our passionate and intimate relationship with the Lord. Discerning with God's character (the heart of God) is so important because many people and leaders are using the written Word of God, the bible, to manipulate and bring people into bondage, some intentionally and others unintentionally, but nevertheless it is being done and we need to know the heart and character of God through Holy Spirit's activity in our lives.

2) What is the fruit that comes from the prophecy, revelation, or supernatural encounter? It should produce fruit that is in line with the Fruit of the Spirit in Galatians 5:22-23, which is God's nature and character. The fruit should draw you closer to the Lord and to His Body, the church. The fruit should produce humility and confidence in the Lord, but it should never produce the spirit of pride and arrogance. It also should never produce an orphan based isolation.

3) In John 16:13, Jesus said that Holy Spirit would lead us into all truth. Also, Romans 8:16 shares that Holy Spirit can bear witness with our reborn human spirit that is born of God according to 1 John 5:1. So what is Holy Spirit saying?

   Beloved, do not believe every spirit, but test the spirits, whether they are of God; because many false prophets have gone out into the world. By this you know the Spirit of God: Every spirit that confesses that Jesus Christ has come in the flesh is of God, and every spirit that does not confess that Jesus Christ has come in the flesh is not of God. And this is the spirit of the Antichrist, which you have heard was coming, and is now already in the world. (1 John 4:1-3)

4) We are commanded to test every supernatural encounter. When we encounter a supernatural being we are commanded to ask it, "Did Jesus Christ come in the Flesh? Before any engagement you

could ask a spiritual being in an encounter, "Did Jesus Christ come in the flesh, die on the cross, shed His blood for the sins of the world and rise again on the third day?" Holy Spirit will tell you how to word the question. Believe me, an angel of the Lord, a Cloud of Witnesses, or Jesus Christ Himself would not be offended if you ask them that question. Now on the flip side, if it is an evil spirit disguising itself, it may just stay there and not say anything, being tortured on the inside as you repeatedly ask this revelatory discerning question. It may also turn back to how it really looks in frustration and anger, or it may just keep talking as if you didn't ask a question. If any of those things take place, you have the power and authority to tell it to leave and go in the name of Jesus Christ. Some angels or heavenly beings will say "Jesus is Lord" or "Jesus has come in the flesh" or something along those lines in the very beginning of the encounter, so there is no delay in this servant of the Lord fulfilling its assignment.

> **SIDENOTE:**   We are in the season where the veil (layer) between the natural and supernatural is at its thinnest, and it is continuing to get thinner.

Engaging in the supernatural Kingdom of God is part of our inheritance as children of God; this is the realm we were born from. We are heirs of God's inheritance, and Jesus Christ, our elder brother is our joint heir and the firstborn of many brethren (that's us). As our blueprint, Jesus only scratched the surface in reflecting the full manifestation of sonship. Below is a list of some functions and titles of Jesus as our big firstborn brother from the dead and how it relates to us, His co-heirs in the Kingdom:

- Jesus is the King of (all) kings
- The Lord of (all) lords
- The High Priest of all priests
- The only begotten Son of God who produced many sons of God

- The Apostle of all who are apostolic
- The Prophet of all who are prophetic

> **SIDENOTE:** The church was established with the convergence of the apostolic and prophetic anointing and functions.

GOD IS THE FIRST

The Apostolic and Prophetic are part of the makeup of God Himself, and because of this, He is the first to operate in the apostolic and the prophetic. When God thinks and imagines something and then speaks it, these words spoken by God prophetically and apostolically converge together, resulting in the creation of what God envisioned and imagined in His mind and heart.

In the beginning, He imagined and thought of man and then produced him in the earth (Genesis 1:26-28).

Eden, the garden of God in the heavenly realm, was reproduced on earth (Genesis 2:8-15).

Mountains were in Heaven and then created on earth (Ezekiel 28:14).

The rainbow was always in Heaven around the throne of God (Revelation 4:3), remaining concealed until God was ready to release it to the earth.

IN THIS SEASON WE NEED BOTH THE APOSTOLIC AND THE PROPHETIC WORKING TOGETHER

So Elijah went from there and found Elisha son of Shaphat. He was plowing with twelve yoke of oxen, and he himself was driving the twelfth pair. Elijah went up to him and threw his cloak around him. Elisha then left his oxen and ran after Elijah. "Let me kiss my father and mother goodbye," he said, "and then I will come with you." "Go back," Elijah replied. "What have I done to you?" So Elisha left him and went back. He took his yoke of oxen and slaughtered them. He burned the plowing equipment to cook the meat and gave it to the people, and they ate. Then he set out to follow Elijah and became his servant. (1 Kings 19:19-21)

This scripture shows the Prophet Elijah calling Elisha into the prophetic ministry as a Prophet. Prior to him encountering Elisha, we see Elisha in the field plowing with twelve yoke of oxen. The number twelve represents complete government and scripture said that Elisha himself was driving the twelfth pair of oxen. It was then that Prophet Elijah went up to him to throw his prophetic cloak of invitation.

Remember when earlier in this book we discovered the ox represents the apostolic and the eagle represents the prophetic? I believe that here we see Elisha first operating in apostolic government (Elisha plowing with the twelve yoke of oxen, and driving the twelfth pair); indicating at that time it wasn't intended for both the apostolic and prophetic to converge together in that season. Thus we see Prophet Elijah coming on the scene to do a prophetic intervention, to realign Elisha to his true calling that God had for him.

Elisha knew from Elijah's mantle that he was being called into the prophetic and not the apostolic. This caused him to leave his oxen and run after the Prophet Elijah. Elijah granted Elisha time to go back to sever his apostolic ties from the past prior to embarking on his new prophetic journey. And the way he severed those apostolic ties was by taking the pair of oxen (the apostolic) "he" was driving, then slaughter them and burn the wooden plowing equipment to cook their meat and feed it to the people. So we see Elisha relinquishing the apostolic government he was attempting to operate in, showing Elijah he will never go back to it by slaughtering the oxen, burning the plowing equipment, and feeding the meat to the people, before proceeding in His God ordained destiny of being a Prophet

But in the season we are now in, the apostolic and the prophetic are merging and converging together as we the church mature and release heaven to the earth, building up the church (members of His household), which is built on the foundation of the apostles and prophets with Jesus being the chief cornerstone.

*Now, therefore, you are no longer strangers and foreigners, but fellow citizens with the saints and members of the household of God, **having been built on the foundation of the apostles and prophets**, Jesus Christ Himself being the chief cornerstone, in whom the whole building, being fitted together, grows into a holy temple in the Lord, in whom you also are being built together for a dwelling place of God in the Spirit.* (Ephesians 2:19-22)

> SIDENOTE: There are things that natural eyes haven't seen and natural ears haven't heard; but they are already prepared in heaven by God and are reserved for this time to be released into the earth.

God commissioned Adam to do what He Himself did: God created a garden (for Adam) eastward in Eden, God's own garden (Ezekiel 28:13). I am paraphrasing, but I can see God telling Adam to "Go and use the provision and supply of Heaven to duplicate and reproduce in the earth what I did."

Humanity may not have realized this, but we have created and implemented many things on earth, that were already in heaven, such as:

- Books
- Throne rooms
- Thrones

These are just a few things man has implemented in the earth that already existed in the Heavenly realm.

DISCERNMENT AGAINST THE COUNTERFEIT FOUR FACE GOVERNMENT

Ezekiel 28 reveals that Satan, aka Lucifer, is a fallen cherub, so he definitely is absolutely disgusted about the revelation of the four face government the cherubim around God's throne carries that ultimately reflects us, the manifested children of God. Satan is absolutely repulsed about that. Below we will see various aspects of the corrupted counterfeit four face government released by the enemy:

COUNTERFEIT APOSTOLIC (THE OX)

Whatever the enemy has stolen from the Kingdom of Light and duplicated in the occult is of great importance to us, the manifested children of God. We the church have to realize that the things the enemy has stolen reveal its great importance and detriment to the kingdom of darkness when they are used with God's original intent. Also, what the enemy claims belongs to him is a counterfeit; therefore, the original is in the Kingdom of God.

Below are several examples:

1) **Translation/Transrelocation:**
   a) Displayed in the Kingdom of God: By Elijah in 1 Kings 18:11-12, Phillip in Acts 8:38-40, By the Apostle Paul in Colossians 2:5, 1 Corinthians 5:3-4
   b) Counterfeit: Astral projection (resembling the stars) and teleportation in the occult
2) **Levitation:**
   a) Displayed in the Kingdom of God: Ezekiel in Ezekiel 8:1-4, and Jesus in Acts 1:9-11 Also, Jesus in Matthew 14:22-33 (Jesus and Peter walking on the water is a form of levitation defying the force of gravity.)
   b) Counterfeit: Levitation in the occult
3) **Stones of fire:**
   a) In heaven are stones of fire, and one of lucifer's functions in heaven before his fall was to walk in the midst of the stones of fire; this is a heavenly function (Ezekiel 28:14)

    b)   Counterfeit: The act of walking on coals in the occult

4) **Headhunting:**

    a)   The Kingdom teaches us that God is our head, which represents authority and our source of strength, power and government. We also realize in the spirit that when we sever the headship of the demonic over a region or person's life, we sever its power and authority over something.

    b)   Counterfeit: The act of taking and possessing a person's head after killing them; whether for rituals and ceremonies for the realms of darkness or to strike fear and intimidation in others which are byproducts of the spirit of fear which brings torment.

5) **Cannibalism:**

    a)   As believers we do not partake in the practice of eating human flesh and drinking human blood, but the revelation and power of this spiritual truth is clearly revealed by Jesus in John 6:47-59 as we spiritually eat His flesh and drink His blood. In verse 51 He shares there is everlasting life given to those who eat the life giving bread from heaven, which is Christ's flesh. We participate in the benefits of spiritually eating Jesus Christ's flesh and drinking His blood through taking communion (Luke 22:17-20, Matthew 26:26-28). In many instances, eating the flesh of Jesus can be represented by eating bread or a cracker, and drinking His blood can be represented in drinking the fruit of the vine, some saints use grape juice or wine. Whatever is used, the importance is that it is done in faith, and intimacy between you and the Lord. I shared this to emphasize that we do not physically eat the flesh and drink the blood of a human being.

    Counterfeit: The practice of eating human flesh and drinking the blood of humans.

COUNTERFEIT PROPHETIC (THE EAGLE)

The enemy also releases the counterfeit prophetic (The Eagle).

Beware of false prophets, who come to you in sheep's clothing, but inwardly they are ravenous wolves. You will know them by their fruits. Do men gather grapes from thorn bushes or figs from thistles? Even so, every good tree bears good fruit, but a bad tree bears bad fruit. A good tree cannot bear bad fruit, nor can a bad tree bear good fruit. Every tree that does not bear good fruit is cut down and thrown into the fire. Therefore by their fruits you will know them. (Matthew 7:15-20)

This warning was from the Lord Jesus. Check it out in the Bible; it is printed in red ink. Graciously, Jesus also gives us the key to detecting the false eagle's face (the false prophetic). We have the word of God as our plumb line to judge. We have Holy Spirit who will lead and guide us into all truth. And we have spiritual eyes to see, to judge the fruit of those who operate in the false prophetic.

> SIDENOTE: In Christ, we not only have discernment against the false prophetic, we also have authority over any demonic force that tries to intimidate or come against us. I thank God for all of my children, and the word of prophecy that is over them. I thank God for my wife's influence, prayers and intercession over them. Only by God's grace, are our children developing and being raised up to see and discern in the spirit. As young eagles, one of them had a dream. In the dream, he was looking out of the house. When he looked over to our neighbor's house, he saw a huge vulture, the size of a human, sitting on their roof. But the instant he gazed upon this birdlike creature it flew away in fear. Then he saw it again and like the first time, once he saw it, it flew away in fear. Thank God, that through God's grace he was able to interpret his dream, and discern that he was seeing the demonic in the spirit. The dream showed the authority he (we) have against unclean spirits, even when they may come looking like a bird, which is scriptural.

ACTIVATION:

So I counsel you to purchase gold perfected by fire, so that you can be truly rich. Purchase a white garment to cover and clothe your shameful Adam-nakedness. Purchase eye salve to be placed over your eyes so that you can truly see. (Revelation 3:18 TPT)

And he took the blind man by the hand and led him out of the village, and when he had spit on his eyes and laid his hands on him, he asked him, "Do you see anything?" And he looked up and said, "I see people, but they look like trees, walking." Then Jesus laid his hands on his eyes again; and he opened his eyes, his sight was restored, and he saw everything clearly. (Mark 8:23-25 ESV)

Meditate on the two above scriptures. Put both of your hands over your eyes; then imagine Jesus laying His hands over your hands, and decree, "I receive the eye salve of the Lord; my spiritual eyes are anointed to see; and I have eyes to see. I believe I receive it. Thank you Lord." Now allow yourself to see Christ laying His hands on your eyes and journal what He says or does.

COUNTERFEIT CHRIST (THE MAN)

*Let no one deceive you by any means; for that Day will not come unless the falling away comes first, and **the man of sin** is revealed, the son of perdition...* (2 Thessalonians 2:3)

*Children, it is the last hour, and as you have heard **that antichrist is coming**, so now **many antichrists have come**. Therefore we know that it is the last hour.* (1 John 2:18)

There are many viewpoints regarding the biblical warning of a man of sin who will come. Many believe he will have a major evil influence in the world, and that he will be the human personification of the antichrist spirit, which is a spirit similar to Christ but opposes the Lord. In the meantime, the enemy has released many antichrist spirits into the world that intentionally influence men and women to oppose us, the Body of Christ.

101

COUNTERFEIT KINGSHIP (LION)

For false christs and false prophets will rise and show great signs and wonders to deceive, if possible, even the elect. (Matthew 24:24)

The coming of the lawless one is according to the working of satan, with all power, signs, and lying wonders… (2 Thessalonians 2:9)

We, the children of God, are called and mandated to operate in the Lion face government as we decree in earth what has already been decreed in Heaven by God, bringing Heaven to earth through our decrees. So it is in the counterfeit, with the false christs and prophets. Followers of the enemy will also speak certain things, and the kingdom of darkness will validate and back up their words to demonstrate great lying signs and wonders to deceive. They will deceive many, but thank God for Holy Spirit, discernment, and our authority as children of God to judge these things.

So that we would not be outwitted by satan; for we are not ignorant of his designs. (2 Corinthians 2:11 ESV)

In the last several years, there has been an intentional convergence taking place between the prophetic and our seer nature (Eagle), the apostolic anointing (Ox), and the kingly anointing of decreeing (Lion). As we mature, we will come to the place of being where we, the Body of Christ, will use the government or anointing of all four faces together. I don't necessarily know how this will fully look.

*And He Himself gave some to be apostles, some prophets, some evangelists, and some pastors and teachers, for the equipping of the saints for the work of ministry, for the edifying of the body of Christ, **till we all** come to the unity of the faith and of the knowledge of the Son of God, to a perfect man, to the measure of the stature of the fullness of Christ; that we should no longer be children, tossed to and fro and carried about with every wind of doctrine, by the trickery of men, in the cunning craftiness of deceitful plotting, but, speaking the truth in love, may grow up in all things into Him who is the head—Christ—from whom the whole body, joined and knit together by what every joint supplies, according to the effective working by which every part does its share, causes growth of the body for the edifying of itself in love.* (Ephesians 4:11-16)

Only God knows how the "till we all" will look and fully function. But I know it will be awesome because we will all come to the unity of faith and knowledge of Jesus, to a perfect and mature body, to the measure of the stature of the fullness of Christ. When Christ was in the earth in the Gospels he didn't and couldn't operate in His fullness. Wow, it is going to be amazing! Praise God! We the church are going to be amazing; and it will only be because of Christ's grace and His glory that transforms us.

SYNERGY OF THE FOUR FACE GOVERNMENTS IN THE EARTH

Below we see the convergent interactions between the true four face governments from heaven, which will produce the synergy (heavenly manifestation) in the earth, through the manifested children of God:

THE EAGLE:

The Eagle which represents the prophetic and our seer nature, ascends into the mountain (government) of God and sees and hears in the heavenly realms those things God wants released and established in the earth.

THE LION:

The Lion decrees in its governmental kingly authority what is seen and heard in the Spirit from the Eagle, then releases it through the power of the decree, to establish it through the power of agreement on behalf of heaven into the earth. The Lion operates as a kingdom legislator in its government.

THE OX:

The Ox represents the apostolic, and this government is necessary to implement heaven's strategy and blueprint in the earth based on those things that have been seen and heard from the Eagle government and decreed by the Lion government.

THE MAN:

The man represents the priesthood of man, operating as a liaison between heaven and earth. It takes a child of God (a human being), who is actually a walking and speaking spirit, made in the image of God, for heaven to work through on the earth. Man's earthly suit (body) is a gateway that gives us God's delegated authority to release and operate in an influential and unique way that spirit beings do not have in the earth without a physical body. God delegated man alone to be the spirit realm's arm (vessel) to manifest through on the earth. That's why the body of man is of upmost importance to the spirit realm (Light and darkness).

Each of the four faces carries a unique sound and frequency in the spirit.

SIDENOTE: The full manifestation of heaven on the earth is locked in the children of God. There can be no full manifestation of heaven on the earth until there is first a fullness of sonship on the earth.

MATURITY: REPENTANCE AND CONTINUAL UPGRADES

*But their minds were blinded. For until this day the same veil remains unlifted in the reading of the Old Testament, because the veil is taken away in Christ. But even to this day, when Moses is read, a veil lies on their heart. Nevertheless **when one turns to the Lord, the veil is taken away**. Now the Lord is the Spirit; and where the Spirit of the Lord is, there is liberty. But we all, with unveiled face, **beholding** as in a mirror the glory of the Lord, are **being transformed** into the same image from glory to glory, just as by the Spirit of the Lord.* (2 Corinthians 3:14-18)

It has been said and is so true that we are transformed as we behold the glory of the Lord; and as we behold the glory, we then become. The glory of the Lord has embedded our key of identity and destiny, and only as we behold the glory of the Lord is that unique key "continually" released upon us and in us, leading to our continual transformation in Christ.

My unique key will not be your key; and your unique key will not be my key. Just as we all have a distinct and special fingerprint and DNA, the same applies to our unique relational identity in Christ. Continual transformation only happens as we continually repent. Repentance, in its simplest meaning, is turning from something to turn towards God. Repentance is also a transformation that comes from turning. Religion has put a negative meaning or feeling towards repentance, saying repentance is only necessary if we are coming into salvation, or if we have sinned or messed up in our walk with the Lord. But this is far from the truth. Yes, repentance is needed in our salvation experience and if we sin, but I am referring here to relational repentance, which is only good and positive to the believer. Based off of Merriam–Webster dictionary, "re" means to go back and do again. So we are to go back to where we came from, remembering we are born again from above. So as we go up to where Christ is, setting our affections on things above, relational repentance is able to take place us in different areas of our walk with God. It is a necessity if one is to go on to maturity because this type of repentance takes us back to our original design that God initially set for our lives. And that my friend, is a continual progressive journey with Holy Spirit.

> SIDENOTE: "Repentance is a sustained (continual) change of thinking about how (our spiritual) reality functions. It is a sustained (continual) change about the nature of (our spiritual) reality." – Justin Paul Abraham

Notice that in *2 Corinthians 3:16* it says, *"When one turns to the Lord."* The word "turns" shows that repentance is something we should continually do. As we turn (in repentance), a veil is taken away. While there is a veil that is removed in the beginning of our walk with the Lord that leads us to Him in salvation, there are other veils in our souls (our mind, memories, will, and intellect), that need to be continually removed as we behold the Lord, and see truth and identity in Him. We then turn from the darkness or blindness that we once had because revelatory light has come into that particular area. This type of darkness or blindness isn't something that will keep us out of heaven or prevent us from being children of God, rather the light of God's glory transforms us to become more like Him; inviting us to live a life more liberated in Him. I believe even our glorified bodies will continue to be transformed to His image throughout eternity, because we will continually behold Him.

That in the ages to come He might show the exceeding riches of His grace in His kindness toward us in Christ Jesus. (Ephesians 2:7)

As we continued to behold Him, the Lord will always reveal something new about Himself to us. Our key of identity that resides in His glory will unlock that new level of glorious transformation in us.

MATURITY: MANIFESTATION OF THE CHILDREN OF GOD

We become what we behold. Along with beholding the Lord Himself, I believe this also involves beholding and receiving those avenues God has established and purposed to bring us to maturity, such as the fivefold ministry and the revelations of the Four Face Government discussed in this book. Also, the seven spirits of God plays a crucial role in our maturity as manifested children of God, along with the convergence of the Four Face Government.

*There shall **come forth** a shoot from the stump of Jesse, and a **branch from his roots shall bear fruit.** And the Spirit of the Lord shall rest upon him, the Spirit of wisdom and understanding, the Spirit of counsel and might, the Spirit of knowledge and the fear of the Lord. And his delight shall be in* *the fear of the Lord. He shall not judge by what his eyes see, or decide disputes by what his ears hear,* (Isaiah 11:1-3 ESV)

The above scriptures speak about the Lord Jesus as the shoot and the branch, and how the seven spirits of God, which are: The spirit of the Lord, the spirit of wisdom, the spirit of understanding, the spirit of counsel, the spirit of might, the spirit of knowledge, and the spirit of the fear of the Lord; all these played a pivotal role in the ministry of Jesus Christ on the earth.

> **SIDENOTE:** When you get an opportunity, read Proverbs Chapter 8 and 9 and listen to what the spirit of wisdom has to say.

Also notice in Isaiah 11:1 that it didn't say the shoot (rod) and branch would just appear, instead it states that a shoot (rod) that will "come forth" and a branch will grow from his roots and "bear fruit," thus showing a time of progression, development and maturity. Then in verse 2, it lays out what will be the cause of this successful "coming forth" of the shoot and "bearing fruit" of the branch, which is the seven spirits of God. Verse 3 also shows us that Jesus will take pleasure and delight in the spirit of the fear of the Lord, and this will also lead Him to a place where He will not judge by what He sees with his natural eyes and what He hears with His natural ears. I think it is important to see the maturation process of our pattern, the Lord Jesus Christ. Let's look at the two public affirmations of the Father over Jesus:

When He had been baptized, Jesus came up immediately from the water; and behold, the heavens were opened to Him, and He saw the Spirit of God descending like a dove and alighting upon Him. And suddenly a voice came from heaven, saying, **"This is My beloved Son, in whom I am well pleased."** (Matthew 3:16-17)

While he was still speaking, behold, a bright cloud overshadowed them; and suddenly a voice came out of the cloud, saying, "This is My beloved Son, in whom I am well pleased. **Hear Him!***"* (Matthew 17:5)

These two accounts show the Father's public affirmations toward Jesus for those present with Jesus to witness. In Matthew 3, the first public affirmation took place during Jesus' water baptism. The Father affirmed Jesus as His beloved son in the presence of John the Baptist, and those who witnessed the baptism. Matthew 4 and other scriptural accounts show that immediately Jesus was led by the Spirit to go into the dessert to be tested by the devil. So we see immediately after this first affirmation that there was a time of testing Jesus had to endure and go through. Not only was Jesus tested in the wilderness after His baptism, there were quite a few times of testing that took place between the Father's two public affirmations of Jesus as His Son. We should also note that between these two public affirmations by the Father, Jesus had many intimate times with the Father on His Mountain (Government), which led to Jesus doing only what the Father showed Him to do, and Jesus saying only what those things Father had Him to say.

Then Jesus answered and said to them, "Most assuredly, I say to you, the Son can do nothing of Himself, but what He sees the Father do; for whatever He does, the Son also does in like manner. (John 5:19)

...though He was a Son, yet He learned obedience by the things which He suffered. (Hebrews 5:8)

During the time and process between both public affirmations, Jesus also learned obedience by the things he suffered. Even though during Jesus' earthly ministry He was the God-man, God set up and designed the master plan, which included Jesus functioning and operating solely as a man who yielded to the Father. Jesus' teachings and actions were under and in the anointing of Holy Spirit.

Remember what we said earlier regarding Isaiah 11:1-3, where it says Jesus would be a shoot (rod) that comes forth from a stomp, and He would also be a branch that grows from roots which will bear good fruit. It was stated earlier that the seven spirits of God: The spirit of the Lord, the spirit of wisdom, the spirit of understanding, the spirit of counsel, the spirit of might, the spirit of knowledge, and the spirit of the fear of the Lord, all played a pivotal role in the ministry of Jesus Christ on the earth. The time between the first and the second public affirmation of the Father would be included in the timeline of Jesus becoming that shoot (rod) that will "come forth"; and as a branch growing as a root, bearing fruit. This period would be a time of progression, development and maturing within His inner man. This is when the government of the seven spirits of God helped bring the man Christ Jesus to maturity, to the point that in the second public affirmation the Father not only affirmed Jesus among Peter, James, John, Elijah and Moses, He also commanded them to Hear Him! The "Hear Him" command of the Father made the second public affirmation distinctly and altogether different. I believe in the second public affirmation on the mount of transfiguration, the Father affirmed a matured Son, as compared to a Son in the first affirmation who still had to be tested. The seven spirits of God played a vital role as Christ matured, and as He submitted to the government of the seven spirits of God.

Now I say that the heir, as long as he is a child, does not differ at all from a slave, though he is master of all, but is under guardians and stewards until the time appointed by the father. (Galatians 4:1-2)

When a human king has a baby son, he and the kingdom view the baby son as a prince, and an heir to the kingdom. But in the area of "carrying endowed authority," at this time the son is no different than a servant of the kingdom. During this time, the father, who is the king, assigns this young son Tutors and Governors to help raise, teach, and prepare this young prince to be a king. During this time of preparation, this young prince continues to grow and mature. As he submits to the process, he will go through tests and challenges; and upon successfully passing them, he will go before his father the king for the bestowing of endowed authority upon him. What is important to remember was during this whole process the prince was always the son of the king, and loved by the king from birth. I would place the ministry of the seven spirits of God, the angels of the Lord and the cloud of witnesses in these categories of Tutors and Governors in Jesus' ministry that helped in His maturing process to where the Father was now able to say "Hear Him."

And there appeared to Him an angel from heaven, strengthening Him in spirit. (Luke 22:43 AMPC)

Then the devil departed from Him, and behold, angels came and minis-tered to Him. (Matthew 4:11 AMPC)

And behold, two men were conversing with Him—Moses and Elijah, Who appeared in splendor and majesty and brightness and were speaking of His exit [from life], which He was about to bring to realization at Jerusalem. (Luke 9:30-31 AMPC)

And Elijah appeared [there] to them, accompanied by Moses, and they were holding [a protracted] conversation with Jesus. (Mark 9:4 AMPC)

The scriptures in the Gospels just capture a snippet of Jesus' full life and ministry. It is very possible that Jesus had many more encounters with the angels of the Lord, and the cloud of witnesses ministering to Him in His Mountain (government). Notice what was revealed and discussed with Jesus as He ascended in His government (Mountain) on the mount of transfiguration. Moses and Elijah were speaking to Jesus about His exit from life, which He was about to actually do in Jerusalem. Also, in Mark 9 it says that Elijah and Moses held a protracted conversation with Jesus in His Mountain. The Merriam-Webster Dictionary defines protracted as "to prolong in time or space." It also means to last longer than anticipated or expected. So in this particular instance it means that the cloud of witnesses or men in white linen, Elijah and Moses "in this scripturally documented scenario" had a long dialogue with Jesus about his death and the things related to His death, burial and resurrection in Jerusalem.

Jesus told Nathanael in John 1:51 that he (Nathanael) would see heaven open, and the angels of God ascending and descending upon the Son of Man. Jesus was stating here that He would continually have angels ascending from Him and descending upon Him, so He continually had the ministry of angels in His life and ministry.

Now the young woman pleased him, and she obtained his favor; so he readily gave beauty preparations to her, besides her allowance. Then **seven choice maidservants** *were provided for her from the king's palace, and he moved her and her maidservants to the best place in the house of the women.* (Esther 2:9)

In the book of Esther, King Ahasuerus appointed seven maidservants to Esther, as she and the other virgins spent twelve months preparing to meet the King. Following this lengthy preparation the King would then decide who his queen would be. Esther 2:12-15 tells us that during this twelve month period, the seven maidservants prepared Esther with oil of myrrh, perfumes, and wisdom; and would advise her on what to do, say and how to act in the presence of the king.

God used the seven maidservants to position Esther for favor. I believe the seven handmaidens represent the seven spirits of God. There were SEVEN maidservants and there are SEVEN spirits of God. And just as the maidservants help prepared and perfect Esther, I believe the seven spirits of God helped mature Christ during His earthly ministry, and they also play a role in maturing us, the Bride of Christ. Jesus is our perfect blueprint and example as our elder, big brother. These seven spirits of God that were interwoven in Jesus' ministry and maturity also desire to be thoroughly interwoven and linked into our ministry and maturity, as manifested children of God in the earth.

John, to the seven churches which are in Asia: Grace to you and peace from Him who is and who was and who is to come, and from the seven Spirits who are before His throne, and from Jesus Christ, the faithful witness, the firstborn from the dead, and the ruler over the kings of the earth. (Revelation 1:4)

In the Apostle John's salutation to the seven churches in the book of Revelation, John sends to them (this also includes you and me) grace and peace from:

1) God, who is, who was and who is to come
2) The seven Spirits of God who are before His throne
3) Jesus Christ, the faithful witness, firstborn from the dead, and ruler over the kings of the earth

It is interesting that the seven Spirits of God are included in sending salutations, grace and peace to the church. It is also intriguing that the revelation of their location to the throne is listed here. God doesn't just insert things in His Word haphazardly; there is always purpose and intent. In the letters (epistles) written to the churches from the apostles such as Paul, John, Peter and James, they included greetings from themselves the writer, and God, including the specificity of the Father, and the Lord Jesus in many salutations. See the example below.

Paul, an apostle of Jesus Christ by the will of God, and Timothy our brother, To the church of God which is at Corinth, with all the saints who are in all Achaia: Grace to you and peace from God our Father and the Lord Jesus Christ. (2 Corinthians 1:1-2)

Here we see the salutation also includes Timothy. These various salutations or greetings included the names of those who had something invested in that church. Timothy was working with Paul during this time period, and he also had ministry invested in the development and success of the church at Corinth. The reason I am mentioning this is because I believe Revelation 1:4 is showing us the importance of the seven spirits of God's ministry in the church.

Immediately I was in the Spirit; and behold, a throne set in heaven, and One sat on the throne. And He who sat there was like a jasper and a sardius stone in appearance; and there was a rainbow around the throne, in appearance like an emerald. Around the throne were twenty-four thrones, and on the thrones I saw twenty-four elders sitting, clothed in white robes; and they had crowns of gold on their heads. And from the throne proceeded lightnings, thunderings, and voices. **Seven lamps of fire were burning before the throne, which are the seven Spirits of God.** *Before the throne there was a sea of glass, like crystal.* **And in the midst of the throne, and around the throne, were four living creatures full of eyes in front and in back. The first living creature was like a lion, the second living creature like a calf, the third living creature had a face like a man, and the fourth living creature was like a flying eagle. The four living creatures, each** *having six wings, were full of eyes around and within.* And they do not rest day or night, saying:

"Holy holy, holy, Lord God Almighty, Who was and is and is to come!" (Revelation 4:2-8)

We see that the seven spirits of God are inclusive in the throne room government of God, and they are very connected to the government of the four face Cherubim around the throne in heaven and in the church, as in the days of Christ on the earth.

The Spirit Himself bears witness with our spirit that we are children of God, and if children, then heirs—heirs of God and joint heirs with Christ, *if indeed we suffer with Him, that we may also be glorified together. For I consider that the sufferings of this present time are not worthy to be compared with the glory which shall be revealed in us.* **For the earnest expectation of the creation eagerly waits for the revealing of the sons of God.** *For the creation was subjected to futility, not willingly, but because of Him who subjected it in hope; because the creation itself also will be delivered from the bondage of corruption into the glorious liberty of the children of God.* (Romans 8:16-21)

When we recognize and start coming into our sonship identity and authority (sonship applies to males and females), as manifested children of God, life on earth doesn't just happen; it begins to respond to us.

DISCUSSION POINTS:

1) How do we, the children of God, relate to the Cherubim in relation to the glory of God?

2) What are some differences between us, the children of God, and the Cherubim?

3) What does 2 Corinthians 3:18 mean to you?

4) Why is Discernment so important?

5) In what scriptural ways can we Discern?

6) How do we test every spiritual encounter?

7) Do you feel having the apostolic and prophetic together is vital for you to be built upon?

8) Why is maturity so important?

9) Did Jesus mature in His earthly ministry? If so, list the things that assisted Him in His maturity.

10) What are the spirits of God listed in Isaiah 11:2-3

CHAPTER 5

GO UP INTO THE MOUNTAIN
IN ORDER TO SIT DOWN

And seeing the multitudes, He went up on a mountain, and when He was seated His disciples came to Him. Then He opened His mouth and taught them, saying... (Matthew 5:1-2)

Throughout the Gospels, Holy Spirit highlights and documents various times throughout Jesus' life and ministry where He continually went up on a mountain to pray and engage the Father. I believe the scriptures only captured a brief snapshot of Jesus getting away and going up on a mountain to pray and engage the Father, and this was a continual part of Jesus' daily walk with the Father.

I really like how the King James Version documents Jesus going up on the mountain throughout the Gospels as "He went up into a mountain."

*And seeing the multitudes, **he went up into a mountain**: and when he was set, his disciples came unto him:* (Matthew 5:1 KJV)

In the earlier part of this book we discussed how mountains and governments are interchangeable, and we also discussed the seat of authority (thrones) on top of the mountain. We will take this further in the life and ministry of Jesus.

RESULTS OF JESUS GOING UP AND SITTING ON HIS MOUNTAIN

Then great multitudes came to Him, having with them the lame, blind, mute, maimed, and many others; and they laid them down at Jesus' feet, and He healed them. So the multitude marveled when they saw the mute speaking, the maimed made whole, the lame walking, and the blind seeing; and they glorified the God of Israel. Now Jesus called His disciples to Himself and said, "I have compassion on the multitude, because they have now continued with Me three days and have nothing to eat. And I do not want to send them away hungry, lest they faint on the way." Then His disciples said to Him, "Where could we get enough bread in the wilderness to fill such a great multitude?" Jesus said to them, "How many loaves do you have?" And they said, "Seven, and a few little fish." So He commanded the multitude to sit down on the ground. And He took the seven loaves and the fish and gave thanks, broke them and gave them to His disciples; and the disciples gave to the multitude. So they all ate and were filled, and they took up seven large baskets full of the fragments that were left. Now those who ate were four thousand men, besides women and children. And He sent away the multitude, got into the boat, and came to the region of Magdala. (Matthew 15:30-39)

The first mention of mountains is in Genesis 8:4, *"The ark rested in the seventh month, the seventeenth day of the month, on the mountains of Ararat."*

So we see in the first instance of a mountain being mentioned in scripture that the "ark" rested on the mountains. The ark rested in the government of the new world, which was to be after the flood.

THE MOUNTAIN EAGLE CONNECTION

Does the eagle mount up at your command, And make its nest on high? On the rock it dwells and resides, On the crag of the rock and the stronghold. From there it spies out the prey; Its eyes observe from afar. (Job 39:27-29)

For you have not come to what may be touched, a blazing fire and darkness and gloom and a tempest and the sound of a trumpet and a voice whose words made the hearers beg that no further messages be spoken to them. For they could not endure the order that was given, "If even a beast touches the mountain, it shall be stoned." Indeed, so terrifying was the sight that Moses said, "I tremble with fear." But you have come to Mount Zion and to the city of the living God, the heavenly Jerusalem, and to innumerable angels in festal gathering, and to the assembly of the firstborn who are enrolled in heaven, and to God, the judge of all, and to the spirits of the righteous made perfect, and to Jesus, the mediator of a new covenant, and to the sprinkled blood that speaks a better word than the blood of Abel. (Hebrews 12:18-24 ESV)

In the natural, eagles rely on mountains for a variety of reasons and benefits. We touched on some of these in Chapter 2 such as:

-   Utilizing the height of mountains to see and prepare for coming storms
-   Using the mountainous viewpoint to look for food and see potential enemies below
-   Using the mountains to assist the eagles in protecting their young, and helping them to raise their young to a place of maturity, where they can take care of themselves

WE ARE AMBASSADORIAL EAGLES

In the spirit realm and in the earth, the Isaiah Company (the eagles) and Mount Zion (the mountain of God) have interdependence with each other to release and manifest heaven to the earth. The Merriam-Webster Dictionary defines interdependence "as the state of being dependent upon one another, and having a mutually dependent relationship." So the Isaiah Company needs engagement in Mount Zion, the Mountain of God (in the heavenly places in Christ which includes Heaven itself). And on the flip side, to have influence in the earth, Mount Zion and Heaven needs engagement with the Isaiah Company, the eagles, born again, prophetic sons and daughters of God, in order to release the heavenly authority into the earth realm.

The Mountain of God, Mount Zion, is comprised of the heavenly Jerusalem, the joyful angels of the Lord, the church in heaven (the cloud of witnesses), we the church on earth, God the Father, and the Lord Jesus Christ. And through the blood of Jesus, we all have the capacity to engage with each other because we are all part of God's community and family in Mount Zion; not only in the future but also in the present NOW.

In Him *we have redemption* ***through His blood****, the forgiveness of sins, according to the riches of His grace which He made to abound toward us in all wisdom and prudence, having made known to us the mystery of His will,* ***according to His good pleasure which He purposed in Himself****, that in the dispensation of the fullness of the times He might gather together in one all things in Christ,* ***both which are in heaven and which are on earth—in Him.*** *In Him also we have obtained an inheritance, being predestined according to the purpose of Him who works all things* ***according to the counsel of His will****...* (Ephesians 1:7-11)

For this reason I bow my knees to the Father of our Lord Jesus Christ, from whom the ***whole family in heaven and earth is named****...* (Ephesians 3:14-15)

An ambassador is a nation's highest-ranking government official (leader) in a foreign nation. His purpose is to represent the government of the land that he or she comes from. The ambassador has unlimited free access to the homeland that he or she represents, especially for councils and board meetings, to discuss strategies and plans, because the ambassador will speak and act on behalf of the leader of the nation he or she represents.

It is important for the ambassador to have access to his or her nation's leader, and vice versa. The ambassador embodies and carries the actual government of the land he or she represents to the degree that wherever the ambassador stands, the ground under his or her feet becomes the sovereignty of the government he or she represents.

Many nations send out ambassadors to other nations to represent and protect their interests throughout the world. In the United States, an ambassador is first nominated by the sitting president and then confirmed by the United States Senate. He or she then serves the President of the United States and at his pleasure. They report directly to the Secretary of State; so this "seat" of authority the ambassador holds and occupies in the government of the United States gives him or her authority to represent the interests of the United States in these other nations. Even when the ambassador is in another nation, that nation honors and respects the authority he or she carries because the seat of authority he or she carries in the United States is the same, even while abroad. So the more powerful the nation's government and military, the more authority that governmental seat carries, causes the ambassador to have more influence.

The same applies to us in regards to being citizens of Heaven. As stated earlier, we are ambassadorial eagles of God, and Mount Zion is the headquarters of the Isaiah Company, the eagles. Philippians 3:20 tells us that our citizenship is in heaven; we are heaven's citizens right now, at this very moment, if we are born again from above.

*Now then, **we are ambassadors for Christ**, as though God were pleading through us: we implore you on Christ's behalf, be reconciled to God.* (2 Corinthians 5:20)

As we ascend and dwell into the heavenly places in Christ through the door, which is Christ, we receive directives from God on what He wants done in the earth. Just as a natural ambassador can have meetings and councils to discuss strategies with the president, we also have the invitation to come up. We have the capacity to have council and board meetings to discuss with God and heaven the strategies He wants released into the earth, whether it's for our family, neighborhood, school system, local governments, state government, national or international government affairs. Also, just like the ambassador's authority in the earth, our authority is a reflection of the seat we have in the spirit realm.

> **SIDENOTE:** The authority you carry in the earth can go no further than the seat (of authority) you sit in, in the spirit.

*But God, who is rich in mercy, because of His great love with which He loved us, even when we were dead in trespasses, made us alive together with Christ (by grace you have been saved), and raised us up together, and **made us sit together in the heavenly places in Christ Jesus**,...* (Ephesians 2:4-6)

ACTIVATION:

I want you to focus on the above scriptures in regards to you being made to sit in the heavenly place in Christ. I want you to engage the Lord and engage the seat of authority He has reserved just for you. Yes, there are times we will lay prostrate before Him as He sits on His throne. But right now, the Lord wants you to accept the throne that He provided for you through His Blood. It's His pleasure that you sit with Him in Heavenly Places. I repeat: It's at His pleasure that you sit with Him in Heavenly Places. Now engage the throne, the seat of your authority, in the Heavenlies. Enjoy the fellowship and the joy of being there with the Lord. You are family and amongst family. Journal what you observe, see and feel.

CHRIST OUR FORERUNNER, THE FIRST AMBASSADOR OF HEAVEN

So Jesus said to them, "Truly, truly, I say to you, the Son can do nothing of his own accord, but only what he sees the Father doing. For whatever the Father does, that the Son does likewise. For the Father loves the Son and shows him all that he himself is doing. And greater works than these will he show him, so that you may marvel. (John 5:19-20)

As Heaven's first and unrivaled ambassador, Jesus Christ showed the importance of His dependence to continually be connected to headquarters (the Father) for directives. Many times before Jesus made any important moves in the earth, he went up into a mountain to pray and engage the Father all night on what to do, and how to do it.

Now it came to pass in those days that He went out to the mountain to pray, and continued all night in prayer to God. And when it was day, He called His disciples to Himself; and from them He chose twelve whom He also named apostles: (Luke 6:12-13)

Jesus knew the importance and the necessity of going up into His Mountain (heavenly government) to engage the Father in Mount Zion.

Let's examine two different instances of people receiving their healings through Jesus' ministry:

1) *Wherever He entered, into villages, cities, or the country, they laid the sick in the marketplaces, and begged Him that they might just touch the hem of His garment. And as **many as touched Him** were made well.* (Mark 6:56)

2) *After this there was a feast of the Jews, and Jesus went up to Jerusalem. Now there is in Jerusalem by the Sheep Gate a pool, which is called in Hebrew, Bethesda, having five porches. **In these lay a great multitude** of sick people, blind, lame, paralyzed, waiting for the moving of the water. For an angel went down at a certain time into the pool and stirred up the water; then whoever stepped in first, after the stirring of the water, was made well of whatever disease he had. Now a certain man was there who had an infirmity thirty-eight years. **When Jesus saw him lying there, and knew that he already had been in that condition a long time, He said to him**, "Do you want to be made well?" The sick man answered Him, "Sir, I have no man to put me into the pool when the water is stirred up; but while I am coming, another steps down before me." Jesus said to him, "Rise, take up your bed and walk." And immediately the man was made well, took up his bed, and walked. And that day was the Sabbath.* (John 5:1-9)

Even though healing manifested in two totally different ways in both of these scriptural accounts, Jesus received his marching orders (directives) from the Father, and he obeyed them. In the first account in Mark, the people's desire and faith played a major role in them receiving healing through their faith (action). Also in this account, Jesus did what the Father directed Him to do by going into those certain villages, cities and countries, and being at the right place at the right time for the multitudes of people to exercise their desire and faith. Prior to Mark 6:56 happening, Jesus received a download of directives from the Father to immediately make his disciples get in a boat, and go to the other side while Jesus went up to His Mountain (government) to engage God.

*Immediately He made His disciples get into the boat and go before Him to the other side, to Bethsaida, while He sent the multitude away. And when He had sent them away, **He departed to the mountain to pray.*** (Mark 6:45-46)

Let us examine the following verses to see the events that transpired involving Jesus and the disciples. We will examine what transpired after Jesus departed "went up into the mountain" or His government. Verse 47 says that evening came, and the boat the disciples were in was in the middle of the Sea of Galilee, possibly around 15 miles from the shore, and Jesus was alone on the land. Verse 48 shows that from up on the mountain Jesus saw them straining and toiling while they were rowing, for the winds were blowing against them. We also notice that it doesn't say that Jesus came down from the mountain (His Government) at any point in this scriptural account. So I believe that Jesus was still in His government as He watched the disciples from a place in His Father's rest.

*Now when evening came, **the boat was in the middle of the sea; and He was alone on the land**. Then He saw them straining at rowing...* (Mark 6:47-48)

The disciples and Jesus were on two different natural terrains and spiritual realms. The disciples were in the boat on the water while Jesus was on the land. While on the water, the disciples were in a spiritual realm of toiling and fear. While on land, Jesus was in a spiritual realm of rest and peace, which was the atmosphere of His Mountain (government).

As we enter into and abide in the rest of the Lord by yielding to Him, God is able to do exceeding and abundantly above all that we can ask or think, in us, and through us. Remember, the disciples are being trained and mentored by Jesus at this point in their lives. Again, in this teachable moment we see the disciples on the water, toiling and straining while Jesus is on land in His government, at rest.

This also applies to us when we are in our mountain (heavenly government). We will be at peace (rest) in the Lord, in spite of whatever challenging circumstances may confront us. Jesus was observing them from his government (mountain) in the fourth watch, which is 3am to 6am. Jesus walked on the water in the Father's rest, walking in authority over the surrounding winds to the point that when Jesus went into the boat the wind instantly stopped and the disciples encountered the government and rest of the Lord, by atmospheric association in verse 51. In verse 53 it says Jesus and the disciples crossed over the Sea of Galilee, into the land of Gennesaret. In John's account in John 6:15-21, verse 21 says the disciples willingly received him (His government of Rest included) into the boat and they were immediately at land on the other side. Once Jesus stepped into the boat in the government of rest, they all, including the boat, experienced supernatural translation and acceleration. The government of rest will also do this in our lives as we yield and willingly receive it into our lives. Jesus walked in His government as he submitted to the directives from the Father, in being at the place that God destined him to be for that day. This led to the people exercising their faith to receive their healing as Christ operated from His Mountain.

The second account in John 5:1-9 shows a man receiving His healing amongst many others who were sick, blind, lame and paralyzed. Why did this one man in this scriptural account receive healing while the multitudes did not? Because the Father showed Jesus what He needed to do in regards to this man receiving his healing. We know that God is good and just. He is not impartial, and He loves us all. The scriptures only give us sneak peeks into what took place, and does not include all the details of the circumstances, or all of the experiences of this man prior to him receiving his healing. It is our job to remember that God is good and God is just!

Righteousness and justice are the foundation of Your throne; Mercy and truth go before Your face. (Psalm 89:14)

Now let us go back to the scripture that we began this chapter with:

And seeing the multitudes, He went up on a mountain, and when He was seated His disciples came to Him. Then He opened His mouth and taught them, saying... (Matthew 5:1-2)

To get the proper context for this passage, let's go back to Matthew 4:23. It shows that Jesus went to Galilee, teaching and preaching the gospel of the kingdom, healing all kinds of sicknesses and diseases. Verse 24 says that his fame went throughout all of Syria, and they brought to Jesus all those who were sick and demon possessed, and Jesus healed them. It ends in verse 25 with multitudes following Jesus from Galilee, Decapolis, Jerusalem, Judea, and beyond Jordan; and this takes us to Matthew 5:1-2. Now seeing the multitudes of people, Jesus went up into his mountain (government), where He engaged the Father in His spirit. It's important to keep in mind that Jesus didn't do these things as God in the flesh, even though He was and is. He submitted Himself to the Father and lived and ministered as a man, surrendering His will to the Father, thus allowing Holy Spirit and the love of the Father to flow and manifest through Him.

And being found in appearance as a man, He humbled Himself and became obedient to the point of death, even the death of the cross. (Philippians 2:9)

Jesus, in Matthew 5, seeing the multitudes, engages the Father in the heavenly realm while still being on earth. He showed us that our spirit man (through Christ) can be in two places at one time.

And no man hath ascended up to heaven, but he that came down from heaven, even the Son of man which is in heaven. (John 3:13 KJV)

Christ went up and sat down on His Mountain (government). Earlier, we discussed the seat of authority and altars that reside on the top of the mountains. Jesus could sit on the seat of authority (throne) on the mountain because He (Jesus) already willingly offered himself on the altar (of

His Mountain), and surrendered the seat of authority to the Father. This surrendering is a continual process that can be clearly demonstrated at various times, we know this at least happened during Jesus' time of fasting, after he was baptized by John the Baptist. After Jesus offered Himself (His will) on the mountain's altar, the Father then takes His full seat on the throne of the mountain of Jesus, heart and soul. Then, after this full surrender, the Father allows Jesus to come and also sit on the seat of authority because the Father can now trust that Jesus will do everything the Father shows Him to do.

> SIDENOTE: Jesus is our perfect, and surrendered blueprint, and Christ as a man had to experience everything we would experience as we surrender to the Father. Therefore, Christ demonstrated to us the perfect example of how the Father desires to treat a surrendered child of God.

Matthew 5:1-2 says that after Jesus went up into the mountain and sat down, he opened His mouth and began to teach from a different realm and government. This is where the famous Beatitudes are issued forth. They are issued out from a different realm because Jesus went up into His mountain (government) and sat down. This surrendering of the soul is so important to our fulfilling the things we were birthed to do for the Kingdom; Jesus was able to go to the cross because He surrendered His will and emotions to the Father.

YOU HAVE A MOUNTAIN (GOVERNMENT)

We also have our individual mountain. Just as Jesus, our forerunner, blueprint, and pattern, had to yield Himself, so must we offer ourselves on the altar of the mountain that we have been destined to live out of. We have to surrender our will, desires, emotions, and everything that could cause opposition or hindrances that reside in our soulish man. That is why renewing our minds is so vitally important. Part of the process of offering ourselves on this mountain's altar is acknowledging, repenting and tearing down any idols that may reside in our souls. We must get rid of the things that God desires for us to let go of; those things that we may want to hold on to; the thing(s) we are giving relevance to, the things that may be in the process of elevating to equal or higher status than God.

Who may ascend the mountain of the Lord? Who may stand in his holy place? The one who has clean hands and a pure heart, who does not trust in an idol or swear by a false god. (Psalm 24:3-4 NIV)

In Psalm 24, the questions were asked, "who may ascend the governmental mountain of the Lord (Mount Zion) and who can stand in His holy place?" The answer is then given, stating it is the one who has clean hands and a pure heart.

If you read it as it stands, you might come away with a performance based mindset; thinking that you need to first have cleans hands before you can get a pure heart. But through believing and receiving the finished work of the cross and the blood of Jesus, we receive a new heart (our spirit man is reborn) "first."

Just like an apple tree can only produce apples and a grapevine can only produce grapes, our new reborn spirit (heart) from God is designed by nature to produce a lifestyle of clean hands, and to not trust in an idol nor swear by a false god. One of the keys to our success is to continually renew our minds in the Word of God as Holy Spirit breathes upon us with revelation. Another important key is our will and desire to do this. When we come to Him in faith, and trust and receive the finished work of the cross of Jesus, which also includes the work accomplished in His burial, resurrection, ascension and sitting down at the right hand of God, the Lord will then do the part that is impossible for us. And that is, purifying our heart (making our spirit man alive again in God). This is something we are unable to do on our own; it took a God, with a supernatural plan, to do that. But after receiving the pure heart through faith in the blood of Jesus first, we then must desire to live a life of clean hands, which will lead to us keeping our heart pure continually. This comes down to our choice and decision to desire, and to have a will to do His will.

SIDENOTE: We must desire and have a will to do His will.

Once we desire and have a will to do His will, God will partner with us, and empower us through the power of Holy Spirit. So our clean hands will be an extension of our pure heart.

For our God is a consuming fire. (Hebrews 12:29)

God's passionate Fire of Love will burn out anything that does not look like Him and anything detrimental to our fellowship with Him, as we willingly yield it to Him just as Christ did.

At each and every sunrise you will hear my voice as I prepare my sacrifice of prayer to you. Every morning I lay out the pieces of my life on the altar and wait for your fire to fall upon my heart. (Psalm 5:3 TPT)

When God sees us put ourselves on the altar of our mountain and surrender our seat of authority to Him, He will invite us to come up to sit on the seat of authority with Him because now He knows that He can trust us. Even though we will be sitting with Him on the seat of authority, He and we both know that HE IS IN CHARGE and HE IS THE KING.

This will enable us to be at work, driving, in the mall, shopping, or anywhere and be able to go up into our mountain, engage God, where we can minister to the needs around us from our mountain (heavenly realm). No one around us would physically know that we engaged God.

As we have discovered, we all have an altar and a seat of authority on our mountain. Whatever is on the altar of our mountain will determine who sits on the seat of authority, the throne of our mountain. Read these two scriptural passages for your engagement:

But Isaac spoke to Abraham his father and said, "My father!" And he said, "Here I am, my son." Then he said, "Look, the fire and the wood, but where is the lamb for a burnt offering?" And Abraham said, "My son, God will provide for Himself the lamb for a burnt offering." So the two of them went together. (Genesis 22:7-8)

Then one of the seraphim flew to me, having in his hand a live coal which he had taken with the tongs from the altar. And he touched my mouth with it, and said: "Behold, this has touched your lips; Your iniquity is taken away, And your sin purged." (Isaiah 6:6-7)

ACTIVATION:

Issac was old enough and he could have easily fought off and resisted an old man like his father Abraham if he desired, but he yielded and willingly put himself on the altar to be a burnt offering to the Lord. In this activation, I want you to close your eyes and engage the Lord. Ask Him, in this engagement, to show you the mountain He has currently given you, and show you the altar on the mountain. I want you to observe that altar and search your heart. Ask God what things He wants you to burn on the altar. These will be things that may be hindering you from going to the next level; they may be things that you really enjoy and love on an equal footing with God or even above Him. God may be asking for you to offer it to Him so He can burn it with His passionate fire. It could be for a season, seasons or permanently removed, keeping in mind God never asks for something without eventually giving something else back in a greater measure. In the spirit, Abraham offered Issac on the altar and God gave us (the world) Jesus. Now in this engagement, when you are ready, I want you to lay on the altar of your mountain. A Seraph will then fly over to you with a live coal in his hand and touch your mouth, which will directly go into your soul and burn up the things God desires to be burned. Journal what you see, feel and observe within this engagement. You may need to do this more than once.

Along with our mountain (government), lies our sphere of influence. Our sphere of influence is an area that has power and authority to affect and influence everything around us. How we steward the mountain and government God has given us will determine how our mountain's influence (government) increases or decreases.

"'Well done!' the king exclaimed. 'You are a good servant. You have been faithful with the little I entrusted to you, so you will be governor of ten cities as your reward.' "The next servant reported, 'Master, I invested your money and made five times the original amount.' "'Well done!' the king said. 'You will be governor over five cities.' "'Yes,' the king replied, 'and to those who use well what they are given, even more will be given. But from those who do nothing, even what little they have will be taken away. (Luke 17:17-19, 26 NLT)

Jesus shows us in this parable that our stewardship, or how responsible we are with what God has entrusted us with, will determine if we increase or decrease in our mountain (government).

In the beginning, Genesis shows us that God gave the Garden of Eden as Adam's mountain (government). It was God's will that Adam's mountain (government) increase from the Garden of Eden and go on to replenish and cover the whole earth, and eventually spread to the whole cosmos. But Adam had to be a good steward and pass the test of stewardship. Sadly, we know that Adam failed the test of stewardship.

And God blessed them. And God said to them, "Be fruitful and multiply and fill the earth and subdue it, and have dominion over the fish of the sea and over the birds of the heavens and over every living thing that moves on the earth." (Genesis 1:28 ESV)

YOUR MOUNTAIN IS CONNECTED TO YOUR BOOK OF DESTINY

We have become his poetry, a re-created people that will fulfill the destiny he has given each of us, for we are joined to Jesus, the Anointed One. Even before we were born, God planned in advance our destiny and the good works we would do to fulfill it! (Ephesians 2:10 TPT)

In the previous chapter, we discovered that we all have a book of destiny that contains everything God has destined for us to do before we came to the earth. Whatever God has destined for us to do in the earth,

He has already given us the grace (the empowerment and ability) and authority to do it.

Jesus also had a book of destiny that was designed specifically for Him before He was born into the earth as a man. Look at what Jesus said about this in Hebrews 10:5-7:

Therefore, when He came into the world, He said: "Sacrifice and offering You did not desire, But a body You have prepared for Me. In burnt offerings and sacrifices for sin You had no pleasure. **Then I said, 'Behold, I have come— In the volume of the book it is written of Me—To do Your will, O God.'"** (Hebrews 10:5-7)

Here we see the writer of the book of Hebrews quoting in verse seven what was prophetically said in Psalm 40:7.

Then I said, "Behold, I come; In the scroll of the book it is written of me." (Psalm 40:7)

Both of these scriptures show us that Jesus' purpose was to fulfill everything that was on His scroll. Contrary to popular belief, I do not believe the book referenced in these two scriptures is referring to the Bible.

And there are also many other things that Jesus did, which if they were written one by one, I suppose that even the world itself could not contain the books that would be written. Amen. (John 21:25)

The Apostle John shared that there were many things Jesus did that were not recorded or documented. If they were, even the world couldn't contain the books, and that would include the Bible. So there are many things Jesus did that are not recorded in the Bible, but all those things are in His Book (Scroll) of Destiny.

Also, just something to think about: The book of Revelation reveals that there is the Lamb's Book of Life which contains the name of everyone who received the blood of Jesus. If Jesus' Book of Destiny and the Lamb's Book of Life are the same book, how amazing and gracious would it be for our names to be written in His Book of Destiny? Again, this is just something to think about. The imagery that comes to mind is of someone, let's say a lady, who has a very special diary. This lady journals in her diary each night. The diary is this lady's escape, and actually something she looks forward to with great anticipation to journal her thoughts, ideas, triumphs, and disappointments. She keeps this diary beside her bed and keeps it locked so no one can just access and read it because it is very personal, private and intimate. In public she is very shy and reserved, but when she journals in her diary she feels free to express herself, so this diary is a reflection of who she truly is, the part of her that she doesn't share with anyone else. In this journal she decides to write the names of the people she loves, adores, and cherishes and beside those names she decides to write something about each person on the list, detailing why she chose them and how they have affected her life for the positive. She then plans to go to each person so they can read the excerpt of what she wrote about them in her diary, choosing to show and share her vulnerability with them. This illustration gives a lower scale idea of what the significance could be if the Lambs' Book of Life is also part of Jesus' book or scroll of destiny and that He has put our names into His intimate book of destiny.

ACTIVATION:

This is a confession to help frame your thoughts and reality in alignment with Heaven. I want you to engage the Lord just by meditating on Him. You could read some of the scriptures that we previously discussed and use them as a door (gateway) for your sanctified imagination. While engaging, I want you to repeat and decree, "Lord, I come into agreement with Heaven and I receive my book of destiny. Lord, if for any reason my book of destiny is closed, I repent and plead the blood of Jesus over anything that is trying to steal, kill or destroy my destiny. And through the blood of Jesus, I come into agreement with the Father's abundant life for me. Lord, open my destiny scroll and allow me to receive the grace and revelation to live out of my book of destiny. Lord, give me clarity and help me to engage you and to hear your voice clearer. I accept and come into agreement with the angels that are assigned to help and assist me in fulfilling my destiny scroll. I believe I receive this, in Jesus' name."

If you can, sit in quietness and meditation for several minutes, then journal what you see, feel and observe.

> **SIDENOTE:** As you do this, you will develop your own words that come out of your inner man to engage with.

WE ARE CHRIST'S SEQUEL IN THE EARTH

"Most assuredly, I say to you, he who believes in Me, the works that I do he will do also; and greater works than these he will do, because I go to My Father. And whatever you ask in My name, that I will do, that the Father may be glorified in the Son. If you ask anything in My name, I will do it. (John 14:12-14)

Jesus did many mighty things during His earthly ministry. He ministered to large numbers of people and taught His disciples many things. But there were also many things Jesus couldn't do or share at that time because the people (his disciples and followers) didn't have the capacity to receive everything that Christ had and is.

I still have many things to say to you, but you cannot bear them now. However, when He, the Spirit of truth, has come, He will guide you into all truth; for He will not speak on His own authority, but whatever He hears He will speak; and He will tell you things to come... (John 16:12-13)

Holy Spirit, the Spirit of truth, empowered the disciples then, and us now, to have the capacity to receive the mysteries and revelatory secrets reserved for us. Later in John 20:22, we see Jesus breathing on His disciples after His resurrection to receive the Holy Spirit, igniting a regeneration and transformation in their spirit man. In Jesus' prayer in John 17, He already said to the Father that the disciples were His and set apart, and because they were His and set apart, the disciples were the first partakers of the regenerating power of Holy Spirit, "after" the cross and resurrection.

And when He had said this, He breathed on them, and said to them, "Receive the Holy Spirit. (John 20:22)

> SIDENOTE: Jesus coming to the earth was so influential in the timeline of humanity that it divides the time before and after his coming to earth. The first half is "BC" or "Before Christ", and the second half is "AD" which is Latin for Anno Domini, or "In the year of the Lord Jesus Christ." Christ's existence on the earth was so pivotal and monumental, that humanity's timeline is influenced and marked by the years that Christ was on the earth. Our status in God is also influenced by the pivotal acts of the Cross and the Resurrection of Jesus Christ. Yes, humanity had a special relationship with God prior to the cross and resurrection of Christ. But after the cross and resurrection, God, through Christ, ushered in a brand new era and new species of people who are in Christ.

The cross and resurrection of Christ opened the gateway for the baptism in the Holy Spirit to come in Acts 2. This assists us in having the capacity to not only receive the revelation of what Christ has done, but also empower us to do the work.

I believe it is the Father's desire for the church and the Bride of Christ to manifest and represent Christ on a higher level than when HE was in the earth during His earthly ministry.

And whatever you ask in My name, that I will do, **that the Father may be glorified in the Son**. *If you ask anything in My name, I will do it.* (John 14:13)

There is more glorification that the Father will receive in the Son (Jesus) NOW, as WE walk in the manifest power of God as the children of God (in sonship). Remember, sonship in this case includes male and female.

I believe that as we mature in this sonship, we will experience and walk in power that has been reserved for us. The angels in heaven and the cloud of witnesses are fascinated by what God is about to do for us, in us, and through us. This authority is connected to the powers of the ages to come.

...and have tasted the good word of God and the powers of the age to come... (Hebrews 6:5)

After we are born again, our physical bodies may look the same; but even with that, many believers through faith are receiving regeneration and rejuvenation in their bodies through the finished work of the cross. If Moses, Caleb and Abraham could operate in supernatural physical rejuvenation, then we also have access. But, as I stated earlier, although our physical bodies may look the same to the human eye, our soulish man (the mind, will, emotions and intellect) is constantly being renewed and transformed by the Word of God. Our reborn spirit man comes from a totally different heavenly realm and age which is beyond this world, called Zion. We discussed Zion earlier in this book.

In our sonship (male and female), God is going to continually lavish us with blessings and His goodness, and we will continually be transformed into His awesome and glorious image for eternity.

But God, who is rich in mercy, because of His great love with which He loved us, even when we were dead in trespasses, made us alive together with Christ (by grace you have been saved), and raised us up together, and made us sit together in the heavenly places in Christ Jesus, that in the ages to come He might show the exceeding riches of His grace in His kindness toward us in Christ Jesus. (Ephesians 2:4-7)

SHHHHHH...CHRIST GAVE US A SNEAK PEAK OF HIM ENGAGING HIS MOUNTAIN!!

Now it came to pass, about eight days after these sayings, that He took Peter, John, and James and went up on the mountain to pray. As He prayed, the appearance of His face was altered, and His robe became white and glistening. And behold, two men talked with Him, who were Moses and Elijah, who appeared in glory and spoke of His decease which He was about to accomplish at Jerusalem. But Peter and those with him were heavy with sleep; and when they were fully awake, they saw His glory and the two men who stood with Him. Then it happened, as they were parting from Him, that Peter said to Jesus, "Master, it is good for us to be here; and let us make three tabernacles:

one for You, one for Moses, and one for Elijah"—not knowing what he said. While he was saying this, a cloud came and overshadowed them; and they were fearful as they entered the cloud. And a voice came out of the cloud, saying, "This is My beloved Son. Hear Him!" When the voice had ceased, Jesus was found alone. But they kept quiet, and told no one in those days any of the things they had seen. (Luke 9:28-36)

I believe the mount of transfiguration's scriptural account provides us a sneak peak of what took many times, or perhaps each time Jesus went up into the Mountain to pray, engaging Mount Zion. We see Him being transfigured to how He really looks in the spirit realm. We also see Him engaging the men in white linen (the cloud of witnesses), Elijah and Moses, and we see the Father coming in His Glory cloud. We know that angels were all around on the mountain during that time. So we saw Mountain Zion in full effect (see Hebrews 12:22-24).

ACTIVATION:

I had a visionary experience with the Lord during a time of engaging Him where He showed me how I looked in the spirit realm. I believe it was how I currently looked in the spirit realm. That's one reason 2 Corinthians 5:16 admonishes us to no longer know our brothers and sisters in Christ after the flesh, but after the spirit, because how we look in the natural is not the way we look in the spirit realm. I was levitating beside the Lord on top of a mountain, and viewing this as if I was the cameraman recording what was going on. It was a panoramic view, and I knew it was me because I recognized my similar facial features, and the glorious light within me was radiating out of my eyes and mouth. I don't share this out of pride because I believe this is all of our inheritance in Christ.

Below are the three scriptural accounts of Jesus' transfiguration on the mountain. I want you to take some time to engage in your reading of these three scriptural accounts, then close your eyes and wait in stillness until you see yourself on the mountain with the Lord as He transfigures before you. Then document in your journal anything else that happens.

1) *Now after six days Jesus took Peter, James, and John his brother, led them up on a high mountain by themselves; and He was transfigured before them. His face shone like the sun, and His clothes became as white as the light. And behold, Moses and Elijah appeared to them, talking with Him. Then Peter answered and said to Jesus, "Lord, it is good for us to be here; if You wish, let us make here three tabernacles: one for You, one for Moses, and one for Elijah." While he was still speaking, behold, a bright cloud overshadowed them; and suddenly a voice came out of the cloud, saying, "This is My beloved Son, in whom I am well pleased. Hear Him!" And when the disciples heard it, they fell on their faces and were greatly afraid. But Jesus came and touched them and said, "Arise, and do not be afraid." When they had lifted up their eyes, they saw no one but Jesus only.* (Matthew 17:1-8)

2) *Now after six days Jesus took Peter, James, and John, and led them up on a high mountain apart by themselves; and He was transfigured before them. His clothes became shining, exceedingly white, like snow, such as no launderer on earth can whiten them. And Elijah appeared to them with Moses, and they were talking with Jesus. Then Peter answered and said to Jesus, "Rabbi, it is good for us to be here; and let us make three tabernacles: one for You, one for Moses, and one for Elijah"— because he did not know what to say, for they were greatly afraid. And a cloud came and overshadowed them; and a voice came out of the cloud, saying, "This is My beloved Son. Hear Him!" Suddenly, when they had looked around, they saw no one anymore, but only Jesus with themselves.* (Mark 9:2-7)

3) *Now it came to pass, about eight days after these sayings, that He took Peter, John, and James and went up on the mountain to pray. As He prayed, the appearance of His face was altered, and His robe became white and glistening. And behold, two men talked with Him, who were Moses and Elijah, who appeared in glory and spoke of His decease which He was about to accomplish at Jerusalem. But Peter and those with him were heavy with sleep; and when they were fully*

awake, they saw His glory and the two men who stood with Him. Then it happened, as they were parting from Him, that Peter said to Jesus, "Master, it is good for us to be here; and let us make three tabernacles: one for You, one for Moses, and one for Elijah"—not knowing what he said. While he was saying this, a cloud came and overshadowed them; and they were fearful as they entered the cloud. And a voice came out of the cloud, saying, "This is My beloved Son. Hear Him!" When the voice had ceased, Jesus was found alone. But they kept quiet, and told no one in those days any of the things they had seen. (Luke 9:28-36)

Journal what you see, hear and observe, as you quiet yourself in stillness before the Lord.

God has invited and commissioned us as ambassadorial eagles to "COME UP and GO!"

DISCUSSION POINTS:

How does stewardship affect the status of our mountain (government)?

Do you know what your mountain (government) is?

Have you asked God to reveal your mountain (government)?

FOOTNOTES:

https://en.wikipedia.org/wiki/Ambassadors_of_the_United_States

CHAPTER 6

INVITATION TO THE ISAIAH COMPANY (EAGLES): COME UP HERE

After these things I looked, and behold, a door standing open in heaven. And the first voice which I heard was like a trumpet speaking with me, saying, "Come up here, and I will show you things which must take place after this." Immediately I was in the Spirit... (Revelation 4:1-2a NJKV)

Years ago, the statement motto for the United States Army was "Uncle Sam Wants You." As intelligent social creatures, God has built inside each of us a yearning to be wanted and a desire to belong. That is one reason why many people join gangs, because they have a sense of belonging and acceptance, along with structure and rules, especially if they did not receive it growing up.

I have some good news. No, actually I have some great news!!! God wants you, God wants me, and He wants us more than we could ever imagine. God actually wants us more than we want Him. You may think to yourself, "But Shawn, I really love the Lord." I am not disputing that, but our love cannot compare to His love for us.

But God demonstrates His own love toward us, in that while we were still sinners, Christ died for us. (Romans 5:8)

We can neither fathom nor comprehend the love God has for us, in spite of how we view it. The desire and passion that God has to be in fellowship with us and us with Him, is unimaginable. Even the angels cannot understand it, seeing the extent that God went to redeem His most prized creation…man (His Children). The Lord loves His angels very much, and we have no idea how long they have been with Him prior to man being created. Job gives an account of the angels rejoicing when God created the earth.

"Where were you when I laid the foundations of the earth? Tell Me, if you have understanding. Who determined its measurements? Surely you know! Or who stretched the line upon it? To what were its foundations fastened? Or who laid its cornerstone, When the morning stars sang together, And all the sons of God shouted for joy? (Job 38:4-7)

The secret place is a place where we can continuously dwell. You can be in a public place, surrounded by people and many voices, but still be in the secret place with the Lord. It's a place of intimacy, oneness and co-union with Christ in God.

Intimacy is God's desire for us to go up and engage with Him. Throughout this book, we have discussed different times and instances where God invited man to come up, such as admonishing us to come boldly before His throne of grace in the book of Hebrews. Below are some other scripture accounts of man engaging with God:

- Adam in the Garden (Genesis 2:15-24, and 3:8)
- Enoch (Genesis 5:24)
- Abraham (Genesis 18:1)
- Jacob saw God (Genesis 28:10-17, and Genesis 32:22-31)
- Moses (face to face encounters in Exodus 33:11)
- Moses and the 70 elders go to heaven, see God, and ate and drank there (Exodus 24:9-11)
- Isaiah (Isaiah 6)

We have two scriptural accounts from the Apostle John who said that no one has seen God, which I believe has been culturally misunderstood by many.

No one has seen God at any time. The only begotten Son, who is in the bosom of the Father, He has declared Him. (John 1:18)

No one has seen God at any time. If we love one another, God abides in us, and His love has been perfected in us. (1 John 4:12)

The person that Holy Spirit is highlighting in these two scriptural accounts is the natural, sinful and un-regenerated man (male or female). This would be a person who is not born again from above, according to John 3:1-18. Also, this person would not be in the Kingdom of Light according to Colossians 1:13. This person cannot even see the Kingdom of God (John 3:3), let alone come into the light (John 3:18-21).

For you are all children of light, children of the day. We are not of the night or of the darkness. (1 Timothy 5:5 ESV)

We, His offspring, are children of light and the light of the world because we have our Heavenly Daddy's nature inside of us. God is Light!

This is the message which we have heard from Him and declare to you, that God is light and in Him is no darkness at all. (1 John 1:5)

BORN OF GOD WHO IS LIGHT

Through scripture we have determined that God is light and we are the children of light. We who are born from above, through faith in the blood of Jesus, are also born of God our Father, Himself.

Everyone who believes that Jesus is the Christ has been born of God, and everyone who loves the Father loves whoever has been born of him. By this we know that we love the children of God, when we love God and obey his commandments. For this is the love of God, that we keep his commandments. And his commandments are not burdensome. For everyone who has been born of God overcomes the world. And this is the victory that has overcome the world—our faith. (1John 5:1-4 ESV)

Having been born again, not of corruptible seed but incorruptible, through the word of God which lives and abides forever. (1 Peter 1:23)

Peter's scripture account reveals to us that when we are born again, we are born again from the incorruptible seed, which is the word of God.

Let us examine the Apostle John's account of seeing God on the throne in Revelation 4:1-11.

*After these things I looked, and behold, a door standing open in heaven. And the first voice which I heard was like a trumpet speaking with me, saying, "Come up here, and I will show you things which must take place after this." Immediately I was in the Spirit; and **behold, a throne set in heaven, and One sat on the throne. And He who sat there was like a jasper and a sardius stone in appearance; and there was a rainbow around the throne, in appearance like an emerald.** Around the throne were twenty-four thrones, and on the thrones I saw twenty-four elders sitting, clothed in white robes; and they had crowns of gold on their heads. And from the throne proceeded lightnings, thunderings, and voices. Seven lamps of fire were burning before the throne, which are the seven Spirits of God. **Before the throne** there was a sea of glass, like crystal. **And in the midst of the throne, and around the throne**, were four living creatures full of eyes in front and in back. The first living creature was like a lion, the second living creature like a calf, the third living creature had a face like a man, and the fourth living creature was like a flying eagle. The four living creatures, each having six wings, were full of eyes around and within. And they do not rest day or night, saying: "Holy, holy, holy, Lord God Almighty, Who was and is and is to come!" Whenever the living creatures give glory and honor and thanks to Him who sits on the throne, who lives forever and ever, the twenty-four elders fall down **before Him who sits on the throne** and worship Him who lives forever and ever, and cast their crowns before the throne, saying: "You are worthy, O Lord, To receive glory and honor and power; For You created all things, And by Your will they exist and were created."*

Psalm 104 states that God is clothed in light as a garment.

*Bless the LORD, O my soul! O LORD my God, you are very great! You are clothed with splendor and majesty, **covering yourself with light as with a garment**, stretching out the heavens like a tent.* (Psalm 104:1-2 ESV)

Every good gift and every perfect gift is from above, coming down from the **Father of lights***, with whom there is no variation or shadow due to change.* (James 1:17 ESV)

Paul also stated in 1 Timothy 6:13-16 ESV, *"I urge you in the sight of God who gives life to all things, and before Christ Jesus who witnessed the good confession before Pontius Pilate, that you keep this commandment without spot, blameless until our Lord Jesus Christ's appearing, which He will manifest in His own time, He who is the blessed and only Potentate, the King of kings and Lord of lords, who alone has immortality, dwelling in unapproachable light, whom no man has seen or can see, to whom be honor and everlasting power. Amen."*

The Orthodox Jewish Bible (OJB) translates "man" in 1 Timothy 6:16 as Bnei Adam. The Orthodox Jewish Bible Glossary defines Bnei Adam as sons of Adam, those of low estate.

In other words, the man (Bnei Adam) referenced in 1 Timothy 6:16 refers to the entirety of mankind that was born from the seed of the fallen, first man Adam. But thank God that the last Adam, the Lord Jesus Christ, has come, and we who are born again with His blood are no longer connected to the fallen Adam of low estate (position and habitation). Instead, we are connected to and IN the last Adam, Jesus Christ, whose estate (position and habitation) is far superior and so are we, because we who are born again from above are IN Christ.

And so it is written, "The first man Adam became a living being." The last Adam became a life-giving spirit.

The first man was of the earth, made of dust; the second Man is the Lord from heaven. (1 Corinthians 15:45, 47)

I really felt led by the Lord to focus more on this area because there has been a massive attack on the church in this area by religious spirits. These demonic entities seek to create a religious mindset that physical death only gives us access to ascend and see God; making death the door and gateway into the supernatural Kingdom realm. Those who believe that death is the only way we can interact with God and heaven have essentially said that death is the force that tore down the wall of separation between God and man. Jesus stated that he is "the" Door, the Way, the Truth and the Life.

I am the door. If anyone enters by Me, he will be saved, and will go in and out and find pasture. (John 10:9)

> **SIDENOTE:**   Jesus said He is the door, and if we enter by or through Him, we will be saved AND we will go IN and OUT and find pasture.

Jesus said to him, "I am the way, the truth, and the life. No one comes to the Father except through Me." (John 14:6)

I hope I have presented a case on who has access and an invitation to approach God's light, and those to whom the light of God would be unapproachable to. Even in regards to these individuals, God's light is not unapproachable because He wants it that way, rather it is only unapproachable to those who refuse to accept the loving invitation of being born again and entering into the Kingdom of His dear Son (The Kingdom of Light). The Father is waiting on us with earnest expectation to believe, accept, and receive the sacrifice of His Son, the Lord Jesus, so He (the Father) can have an intimate relationship and fellowship with us.

Jesus answered, If a person [really] loves Me, he will keep My word [obey My teaching]; and My Father will love him, and We will come to him and make Our home (abode, special dwelling place) with him. (John 14:23 AMPC)

If you are a believer and never before realized that you could engage God in a deeper supernatural way, I would encourage you to talk to God and repent, which means to change your thinking and your perception of how you see yourself in Christ.

Paul encourages us to set our affections and passions on things above rather than on the temporal things on this earth.

If then you have been raised with Christ [to a new life, thus sharing His resurrection from the dead], aim at and seek the [rich, eternal treasures] that are above, where Christ is, seated at the right hand of God. And set your minds and keep them set on what is above (the higher things), not on the things that are on the earth. For [as far as this world is concerned] you have died, and your [new, real] life is hidden with Christ in God. (Colossians 3:1-3 AMPC)

God has called and given the invitation for all of us to be eagles, the greatest of the fowls of the air.

What determines whether we are eagles, tree top birds, or land birds like chickens or domesticated turkeys is our desire, our knowledge, or lack of knowledge. Only an eagle can teach an eagle; and the same is true for the lion, ox and man.

Holy Spirit is the revealer of each one. Just as Jesus in His flesh depended on and yielded to Holy Spirit, so must we if we are to soar to the highest heights God where intended us to be.

ENDNOTE:

https://www.biblestudytools.com/ojb/

CHAPTER 7

ENGAGEMENT AND ACTIVATIONS

I want to leave you with some scriptures that you can use in your devotion time with the Lord. Below will be exercises you can use as you focus and meditate on framing images in your sanctified imagination.

Holy Spirit will nudge you, prompt you, and even wake you up for fellowship with the Lord. It also involves our desire and participation. We all have different schedules in the day and night, but with your desire, hunger and participation, the Lord desires and will set up time with just you and Him together. Jesus had special times with the Father, very early in the morning:

After He had dismissed the crowds, He went up on the mountain by Himself to pray. When it was evening, He was there alone. But the boat [by this time] was already a long distance from land, tossed and battered by the waves; for the wind was against them. And in the fourth watch of the night (3:00-6:00 a.m.) Jesus came to them, walking on the sea. (Matthew 14:23-25)

Meditate on the below scriptures and use the Word as a door to step into a closer relation with Him. Remember, Jesus Christ is the door and access point; so use the Word to rest totally in Him.

ENTER INTO HIS REST

There remains therefore a rest for the people of God. For he who has entered His rest has himself also ceased from his works as God did from His. (Hebrews 4:9-10)

ENGAGEMENT 1:

The Lord is my shepherd; I shall not want. He makes me to lie down in green pastures; He leads me beside the still waters. He restores my soul; He leads me in the paths of righteousness For His name's sake. Yea, though I walk through the valley of the shadow of death, I will fear no evil; For You are with me; Your rod and Your staff, they comfort me. You prepare a table before me in the presence of my enemies; You anoint my head with oil; My cup runs over. Surely goodness and mercy shall follow me All the days of my life; And I will dwell in the house of the Lord Forever. (Psalm 23)

MOUNTAINS (GOVERNMENT)

We have an invitation to go up into our Mountain because of our seat of authority in Heavenly Places in Christ.

ENGAGEMENT 2:

After these things I looked, and behold, a door standing open in heaven. And the first voice which I heard was like a trumpet speaking with me, saying, "Come up here, and I will show you things which must take place after this." (Revelation 4:1)

ENGAGEMENT 3:

But you have come to Mount Zion and to the city of the living God, the heavenly Jerusalem, to an innumerable company of angels, to the general assembly and church of the firstborn who are registered in heaven, to God the Judge of all, to the spirits of just men made perfect, to Jesus the Mediator of the new covenant, and to the blood of sprinkling that speaks better things than that of Abel. (Hebrews 12:22-24)

ENGAGEMENT 4:

The earth is the Lord's, and all its fullness, The world and those who dwell therein. For He has founded it upon the seas, And established it upon the waters. Who may ascend into the hill of the Lord? Or who may stand in His holy place? He who has clean hands and a pure heart, Who has not lifted up his soul to an idol, Nor sworn deceitfully. He shall receive blessing from the Lord, And righteousness from the God of his salvation. This is Jacob, the generation of those who seek Him, Who seek Your face. Selah Lift up your heads, O you gates! And be lifted up, you everlasting doors! And the King of glory shall come in Who is this King of glory? The Lord strong and mighty, The Lord mighty in battle. Lift up your heads, O you gates! Lift up, you everlasting doors! And the King of glory shall come in. Who is this King of glory? The Lord of hosts, He is the King of glory. Selah (Psalm 24)

ENGAGEMENT 5:

Have you not known? Have you not heard? The everlasting God, the Lord, The Creator of the ends of the earth, Neither faints nor is weary. His understanding is unsearchable. He gives power to the weak, And to those who have no might He increases strength. Even the youths shall faint and be weary, And the young men shall utterly fall, But those who wait on the Lord Shall renew their strength; They shall mount up with wings like eagles, They shall run and not be weary, They shall walk and not faint. (Isaiah 40:28-31)

Engagement 6:

Now it shall come to pass in the latter days That the mountain of the Lord's house Shall be established on the top of the mountains, And shall be exalted above the hills; And all nations shall flow to it. Many people shall come and say, "Come, and let us go up to the mountain of the Lord, To the house of the God of Jacob; He will teach us His ways, And we shall walk in His paths." For out of Zion shall go forth the law, And the word of the Lord from Jerusalem. (Isaiah 2:1-3)

In your imagination see yourself going up into the Mountain (Government) with Jesus

Engagement 7:

And when he had sent the multitudes away, he went up into a mountain apart to pray: and when the evening was come, he was there alone. (Matthew 14:23 NJKV)

And it came to pass in those days, that he went out into a mountain to pray, and continued all night in prayer to God. (Luke 6:12 KJV)

And Jesus went up into a mountain, and there he sat with his disciples. (John 6:3)

Transfigured with Him in the Mountain

Exercise 8:

Now after six days Jesus took Peter, James, and John his brother, led them up on a high mountain by themselves; and He was transfigured before them. His face shone like the sun, and His clothes became as white as the light. And behold, Moses and Elijah appeared to them, talking with Him. Then Peter answered and said to Jesus, "Lord, it is good for us to be here; if You wish, let

*us make here three tabernacles: one for You, one for Moses, and one for Elijah."
While he was still speaking, behold, a bright cloud overshadowed them; and
suddenly a voice came out of the cloud, saying, "This is My beloved Son, in
whom I am well pleased. Hear Him!" And when the disciples heard it, they
fell on their faces and were greatly afraid. But Jesus came and touched them
and said, "Arise, and do not be afraid." When they had lifted up their eyes,
they saw no one but Jesus only.* (Mark 9:2–8)

SITTING ON YOUR SEAT OF AUTHORITY WITH CHRIST

EXERCISE 9:

*But God, who is rich in mercy, because of His great love with which He
loved us, even when we were dead in trespasses, made us alive together with
Christ (by grace you have been saved), and raised us up together, and made
us sit together in the heavenly places in Christ Jesus, that in the ages to come
He might show the exceeding riches of His grace in His kindness toward us in
Christ Jesus.* (Ephesians 2:4-7 NJKV)

EXERCISE 10:

*If then you were raised with Christ, seek those things which are above,
where Christ is, sitting at the right hand of God. Set your mind on things
above, not on things on the earth. For you died, and your life is hidden with
Christ in God. When Christ who is our life appears, then you also will appear
with Him in glory.* (Colossians 3:1-4)

ENGAGING THE HEAVENLY REALMS IN CHRIST

EXERCISE 11:

In the year that King Uzziah died, I saw the Lord sitting on a throne, high and lifted up, and the train of His robe filled the temple. Above it stood seraphim; each one had six wings: with two he covered his face, with two he covered his feet, and with two he flew. And one cried to another and said: "Holy, holy, holy is the Lord of hosts; The whole earth is full of His glory!" And the posts of the door were shaken by the voice of him who cried out, and the house was filled with smoke. So I said: "Woe is me, for I am undone! Because I am a man of unclean lips, And I dwell in the midst of a people of unclean lips; For my eyes have seen the King, The Lord of hosts." Then one of the seraphim flew to me, having in his hand a live coal which he had taken with the tongs from the altar. And he touched my mouth with it, and said: "Behold, this has touched your lips; Your iniquity is taken away, And your sin purged." Also I heard the voice of the Lord, saying: "Whom shall I send, And who will go for Us?" Then I said, "Here am I! Send me." (Isaiah 6:1-8)

EXERCISE 12:

After these things I looked, and behold, a door standing open in heaven. And the first voice which I heard was like a trumpet speaking with me, saying, "Come up here, and I will show you things which must take place after this." Immediately I was in the Spirit; and behold, a throne set in heaven, and One sat on the throne. And He who sat there was like a jasper and a sardius stone in appearance; and there was a rainbow around the throne, in appearance like an emerald. Around the throne were twenty-four thrones, and on the thrones I saw twenty-four elders sitting, clothed in white robes; and they had crowns of gold on their heads. And from the throne proceeded lightnings, thunderings, and voices. Seven lamps of fire were burning before the throne, which are the seven Spirits of God. Before the throne there was a sea of glass, like crystal. And in the midst of the throne, and around the throne, were four living creatures full of eyes in front and in back. The first living creature was like a lion, the second living creature like a calf, the third living creature had a face like a man, and the fourth living creature was like a flying eagle. The four living creatures, each having six wings, were full of eyes around and within. And they do not rest day or night, saying: "Holy, holy, holy, Lord God Almighty, Who was and is and is to come!" Whenever the living creatures give glory and honor and thanks to Him who sits on the throne, who lives forever and ever, the twenty-four elders fall down before Him who sits on the throne and worship Him who lives forever and ever, and cast their crowns before the throne, saying: "You are worthy, O Lord, To receive glory and honor and power; For You created all things, And by Your will they exist and were created." (Revelation 4)

EXERCISE 13:

In the thirtieth year on the fifth day of the fourth month, as I was among the exiles by the river Chebar, the heavens opened, and I saw visions of God. I looked, and behold, a storm wind came from the north, a great cloud with flashing fire and brightness all around it, and something like a glowing alloy out of the fire. From within it came the likeness of four living creatures. This was their appearance: they had a likeness of a human, but each one had four faces and each one of them had four wings. Their legs were straight and the soles of their feet were like the hoof of a calf. They sparkled like the color of burnished bronze. They had human hands under their wings on their four sides. The four of them had faces and wings: their wings touched one another; they did not turn when they moved; each could move in the direction of any of its faces. As for the form of their faces, each had a human face, the four had the face of a lion on the right side, the four had the face of an ox on the left side and the four had the face of an eagle. Such were their faces. Their wings were spread out above. Each creature had two wings touching the wing of another, while another two were covering their bodies. Now each being could move in the direction of any of its faces; wherever the Ruach would go, they went, without turning as they went. As for the form of the living creatures, their appearance was like burning coals of fire, resembling torches moving between the living creatures. There was brightness to the fire, and lightning went forth from the fire. The living creatures were running back and forth like flashes of lightning. As I looked at the living creatures, behold, one wheel was on the ground next to each of the four-faced creatures. The appearance and structure of the wheels was like the gleaming of beryl. The four had the same likeness, their appearance and their structure seemed to be a wheel within a wheel. When they went, they went in any of their four directions without pivoting as they went. Their rims were high and awesome—all four rims were full of eyes all around. When the living creatures went, the wheels went beside them. When the living creatures rose from the earth, the wheels rose. Wherever the Ruach wanted to go, they went, in the direction the Ruach wanted to go. The wheels rose along with them, for the spirit of the living creatures was in the wheels. Whenever the creatures went, the wheels went. When the creatures stood still, these wheels stood still. When the creatures rose from the earth, the wheels rose with them, for the spirit of the living creatures was in the wheels. Now over the heads of the living creatures there was something like an expanse, shining like the color of ice, stretched forth over their heads. Under the expanse, their wings were stretched out straight, one toward the other. Each had another pair covering its body. When they moved, I could hear the sound of their wings like the sound of rushing waters, like the voice of Shaddai, a noise of tumult like the noise of an army. Whenever they stood still, they let down their wings. There came a voice from above the expanse over their heads. Whenever they stood still, they let down their wings. Above the expanse over their heads was something like a throne, resembling a sapphire stone. Above the shape of the throne was a figure of human appearance. From what appeared as his waist upward, I saw a glowing metal, looking like a fire encased in a frame. From what was like his waist down, I saw the appearance of fire radiating around him. Like the appearance of the rainbow in the cloud on a rainy day, so was the appearance of the radiance. It was the appearance of the likeness of the glory of ADONAI. I saw it, fell upon my face, and heard the voice of the One who was speaking. (Ezekiel 1:1, 4-28)

LOVING ENCOURAGEMENT: FAMILY TALK

Earlier in this book in Chapter 4: *Convergence and Synergy of the Four Face Government*, we touched on the importance of having clean hands and a pure heart, and the important role that our desires play in this. I also want to say that the baptism and empowering of Holy Spirit according to Acts 2 are so powerful and important in our supernatural journey on earth.

The baptism of the Holy Spirit is a baptism for believers (sons and daughters), and its function is not to save you because you already have the seed of God inside of you through believing the gospel, and repenting (turning back to the Lord). Instead, it empowers the believer to have clean hands 'with power'. This by no means is intended to bring any condemnation to my brothers and sisters who haven't received the baptism of Holy Spirit according to Acts 2, but only a loving encouragement to receive it.

In your personal time with the Lord, ask and seek God's heart on this issue and be sensitive to what He says or shows you, or who He allows to come across your path that may share more about this topic. Even if we cannot articulate our heart's desires in words, God will send an answer to our heart's cry because He's a good Daddy. Also, for those who may have already experienced the baptism of Holy Spirit according to Acts 2, do not be content and complacent; Continually desire and seek to ascend and go higher as an eagle, always going deeper in Him in humility, because the humility door to more is in the floor.

| SIDENOTE: "The Door is in the Floor" – Justin Paul Abraham

Also, let me conclude by saying this: If you have believed and received the finished work of the Cross of Christ but you disagree with my view of the baptism of Holy Spirit according to Acts 2, being a son's blessing of inheritance and a daughter's blessing of inheritance, we are still God's family (sons and daughters) and loved. And as God's family, we have the power to agree or disagree and see things differently, but I challenge you to ask Him to show you His heart on this matter. I love you much!

In Jesus' Service,

BIBLE TRANSLATION COPYRIGHTS

RECOMMENDED RESOURCES

Below are two companion resources to this book.

YOU ARE BETHEL, A GATEWAY OF HEAVEN

In this MP3 profound message, *You are Bethel, a gateway of Heaven*, Shawn Easton shares how Ladders, Doorways and Gateways are part of your supernatural DNA in Christ. The truths on this Mp3 sets a foundational precedent for Heaven to release its resources through you into the earth as a portal. It's taught with anointed piano instrumental music playing softly in the background by DappyTKeys.

A companion resource for this book.

www.4xcovergence.com

SOAKING IN THE HEAVENLY
4 FACE IDENTITY

This MP3, *Soaking in the Heavenly 4 Face Identity,* is full of interactive and engaging activations with the sole purpose of engaging the Lord in the heavenly places, the place that our born again spirit is born from. These soaking sessions will create the atmosphere to engage the Lord and the heavenly realms with your sanctified imagine as you continue to develop your spiritual senses through practice, and stillness. As you engage in these activations, anointed piano instrumental music plays softly in the background by DappyTKeys. Get ready for activation!!!

This resource is recommended to be used after reading this book.

www.4xcovergence.com

THE PROSPERITY SERIES

To understand perfect God's will on any particular area, you must get His Word down on the inside of your heart. We have gathered scriptures in the subjects listed below on MP3s and CD's. The scriptures are read aloud as soothing, anointed, piano instrumental music plays softly in the background ministered by DappyTKeys as you feed your spirit with God's Word and renew your mind in the following areas:

Spiritual Prosperity (Part of the *3 John 2 Package*)

Healing and Wholeness (Part of the *3 John 2 Package*)

Financial Prosperity and Successful Kingdom
Entrepreneurship (Part of the *3 John 2 Package*)

Kingdom Babies and Children

Play the Word over babies and children; this resource
is perfect for them as they sleep

Kingdom Marriages

This resource will assist your marriage as you
continue to renew your mind in this area

Kingdom Parenting (Raising young royalty)

It can be quite challenging raising children in these times, this resource will help you with the wisdom of God in this area as you seek to raising Godly children.

Kingdom Singleness

This resource will bless the singles as they serve God with unhindered passion and wisdom

The Warfare of Praise and Worship

This resource will create an atmosphere of praise, worship and Kingdom warfare in your life

Other Books by Shawn Easton

Divine Connections

www.4xcovergence.com

Also visit our website and subscribe to join our community of fellow Becomers on our blog *The Journey of Flowing and Becoming*

For contact and further information and updates visit 4Xconvergence.com

ABOUT THE AUTHOR

Shawn Easton, loves spending time with the Lord and with his family. He is the founder of 4xConvergence, a kingdom business that serves in helping to bring people to their true Identity in Christ, through though-provoking resources. Shawn is a husband, father, entrepreneur, blogger, teacher, a credentialed Biblical Life Coach, and most of all a son of God. He is the author of "Divine Connections "and will be releasing "Eagles and Mountains Volume 2" in the near future, he is just grateful for the grace of God that is on his life. A third generation believer, Shawn is very blessed and driven to fulfill the mandate of the Lord over his life along with his wife, and to pass it down to his generation. Since 2015 he has been on a spiritual journey of intimacy with the Lord exploring the vastness of transformational sonship. He lives in Maryland with his beautiful wife, Keisha, and anointed twin boys, and love spending time with his family.

Made in the USA
Monee, IL
02 October 2020